# Praise

## *The Gift of S*

C000217365

Humanity is experiencing a slow, sometimes painful, shift in consciousness. Of course, from a larger perspective, it all happens in the blink of a cosmic eye. Change is no longer at hand but fully underway as the norms that hold our world slowly dissolve. The word 'unprecedented' is being used unprecedentedly.

One of these important changes is the understanding of human emotions. In a world that has been based on survival of the fittest, we now see an awaking to the reality of the gifts of sensitivity. People who have had to learn to toughen up to get ahead are now leaning toward the gifts of highly sensitive people. Once seen as a detriment, emotions are now emerging as a powerful attribute.

In *The Gift of Sensitivity*, Elena Amber takes us through these hidden gifts of sensitivity and shows us practical ways to channel these to their highest levels. This is a guidebook for the evolving new peoples of planet Earth.

Well done, Elena; we need this now more than ever!

**Steve Rother**, Founder, speaker, 8x author and 5x presenter at the United Nations, including The Class on Channeling

Sensitivity and empathy are core skills for experienced designers. In this highly personal work, Elena Amber shares the tale of how she became more sensitive, and the benefits of sensitivity.

**James Wallman**, Futurist, 2x TEDx, 2x bestselling books, CEO, World Experience Organization

In *The Gift of Sensitivity*, Elena Amber offers us a deep shift in perception as she invites us back to what I consider the greatest of all human capacities … the gift of our sensitivity. To fully embrace our sensitivity changes are relationship to ourselves, expands our reality, and gives us permission to walk in this world as the love that we truly are! We live at a time when we really must embrace what we have access to and let that shine as new potentials and possibilities. If you struggle with your sensitivity and what you access because of it, read this book. You'll be glad you did!

**Suzy Miller**, Founder and CEO at Blue Star Education and Research, author of *Awesomism: A New Way to Understand the Diagnosis of Autism*

Life is a process of change, and Elena Amber invites us to embrace it. Her journey of emotional mastery, helped her navigate through her life's odyssey and like Ulysses find her Ithaka, her heart. She is opening up about her own life and how disconnecting from her emotions led to experiencing personal and professional hardships. One could say that the book is written as an autobiography, revealing the author's struggles to find her place in her own family and society ... to find her true self. *The Gift of Sensitivity* invites the reader to let part of their 'ego' dissolve, connect with their core, enjoy everything they do, and master their lives without being afraid to be sensitive, understand others, show empathy, and be vulnerable. Instead of disconnecting from emotions, which is a common practice in the business world, Elena Amber urges us to listen to our emotions and use them as a compass for our work and life's decisions and direction. I am willing to try it and know the process will be rewarding.

**Dr. Ioanna Papasolomou**, Professor,
University of Nicosia School of Business, Cyprus

Elena Amber has a remarkable skill in defining and explaining conditions, states of being that have taken me 25 years to figure out for myself ... but that I have never had the right words to explain to others! Thank her for 'verbalizing' such things. To add what I hope may be valuable to others here, I sometimes use the old English idiom of 'maintaining a sunny disposition' to help others when the dark days descend upon them as well as 'keep one's perspective' (or for the robust there is the Monty Python 'Life of Brian' song!). Still, these mere words lack the empathy Elena seems able to deliver. It is not my field of work to wonder amongst the tangled emotions of others, but I do recognize those who have a talent in this area. I wish Elena to stay well and keep doing what she does!

**Antony Abell**, CEO & Co-Founder, TrustMe™ / TPX™
Property Exchanges Group of Companies, London

Elena Amber's work on sensitivity is important, especially in the era of our society's collective empathy deficit. If you're an empath, reading *The Gift of Sensitivity* will feel like a balm to your soul.

**Anita Nowak,** PhD, author of *Purposeful Empathy: Tapping Our Hidden Superpower for Personal, Organizational, and Social Change*

This inspiring book takes readers on a rollercoaster journey through the author's life, starting from a fragile childhood and leading to a successful business career, scientific research, and spiritual exploration. The author demonstrates the human spirit's capacity to learn and grow from life's challenges throughout the book. What sets this book apart is its emphasis on the hidden power of emotional engagement as the key to actions. The concept of 'emotional nested baskets' is particularly insightful. Overall, this is an encouraging read for anyone seeking to understand themselves better and tap into their inner resources.

**Aksinya Samoylova**, Talent Angel, author of *Why Polymaths?*

# The gift of sensitivity

## The extraordinary power of emotional engagement in life and work

**Elena V. Amber**

Foreword by
Paul J. Zak

First published in Great Britain by Practical Inspiration Publishing, 2023

The moral rights of the author have been asserted

ISBN    9781788605021 (print)
            9781788605014 (epub)
            9781788605007 (mobi)

Every effort has been made to trace copyright holders and to obtain their permission for the use of copyright material. The publisher apologizes for any errors or omissions and would be grateful if notified of any corrections that should be incorporated in future reprints or editions of this book.

Want to bulk-buy copies of this book for your team and colleagues? We can customize the content and co-brand *The Gift of Sensitivity* to suit your business's needs.

Please email info@practicalinspiration.com for more details.

Discover a new perspective on the purpose of our existence in this captivating book.

We are not meant to simply stumble through a never-ending cycle of trial and error.

In fact, experience may not be the key at all. Instead, let's focus on freeing ourselves from the emotional burdens that come with these experiences.

It's time to shift our attention from external outcomes to the profound world within us – a hidden force that shapes our lives.

Prepare to embark on a transformative journey towards emotional liberation, heightened sensitivity, and the limitless potential that awaits.

# Contents

# Preface

The idea to make the world a better place or humans a better race is twofold: on the one hand, we could change it endlessly for what we believe is good, and on another, we could shift our perception to accept it and fall in love with reality.

The world is individually perceived; some find it fantastic, yet some can barely cope. The truth is that how you perceive it will continue. If you find it harsh, the chances you could get in touch with stress, depression, loneliness, disintegration, and polarization of the current social world are pretty high. Our perception is highly selective and individual, and we are attuned to particular things. What we pay attention to becomes augmented for us, and we increasingly start to see it, as it would be resonating at the same frequency. Therefore, it is better to notice where we put our attention.

To manage attention, many choose ongoing control of their state and thoughts via mindfulness techniques. In my case, mental choices and willpower to direct attention were useless because they were disconnected from my emotions and bodily sensations. I was born as a member of the population that science calls 'highly sensitive people.' This means I see, taste, hear, smell, and feel many more stimuli than others, and I feel them more intensely. High sensitivity is an innate trait, so I could not choose what to sense or feel, streaming it maximally, as many sensitives or empaths do. In the pursuit to become 'normal,' I realized that self-control of attention caused a disconnection from my emotions which became a process of self-destruction.

However, I have made a breakthrough using self-care and compassion and found a way to liberate myself without denying the truth about my emotional states. In this book, I share the details of my journey and understanding of how a connection to emotions enables us to release self-control or any other type of control, uniting with our inner world. These are emotions that polarize our thoughts, making them good, bad, or neutral, so why do we control thoughts instead of releasing emotions? As proven by neuroscience, perception and attention are managed by an emotional engagement prioritizing what is emotionally important to us. Processing emotional states help us to heal vulnerability, get clarity, and tap into the gift of sensitivity by nourishing our innate faculties for healthy emotional engagement.

As a next step, I dealt with socially accepted but limiting beliefs serving many. For example, a chain of events in my life pushed me to question the well-known notion that we are here to learn from experience. I doubted this because of the repetitive pattern of losing people dear to me, which brought me to severe depression, the abyss of pain, and health problems, without allowing me to understand what and how I could learn more. This experience made me a researcher into this subject, and I now suggest that we are here not to get more but to get rid of such experiences or, to be precise, of their emotional consequences. In the same way, I questioned other concepts, such as 'the hero's journey' or 'the need to become a better version of self every day.' In my observations, I found that when we act despite our inner states, we often burn out, so our mentally driven achievements could be at the cost of our health and well-being following unnecessary life tensions.

Instead of disconnections that became a norm from my business executive experience and going through enormous fear, I decided to connect with my emotions and sensitivity more profoundly. Instead of separating from and working against my nature, I embraced it with blind faith that it must have a reason and dived into the unknown emotional subconscious. I took a step away from attention management and focused on emotional engagement, which, in turn, has the superpower to drive perception and attention. Mind techniques, therefore, were combined with heart faculties, where awareness of emotions was necessary but only the initial step. I conclude that awareness, which is offered by mindfulness, is only the preliminary step regarding our inner emotional states where we could not liberate without full acceptance. However, I needed to learn that mental acceptance doesn't work, and found a way to complete transformations.

I didn't make tens or hundreds of emotional release sessions. I have practiced for eight years to ensure it works with hard evidence. In addition to my psychological practice, I became the preceptor of Heartfulness meditation, delved into the measurement tools of neuroscience, studied prolonged exposure therapy, and started my Ph.D. research on emotional engagement. I tested biological data of my own body, such as brain wave activity and emotional engagement, checked individual psychological safety, researched hundreds of emotions-related articles and books in science and spirituality, did psychological tests on life satisfaction and well-being, and enacted a journaling of life events. My experiment suggests that the direction of attention necessarily follows once the emotional attachment is released, so we alter our perception without needing to control our thoughts or be aware of our emotional states anymore; we transform them. The blend of deep meditative practice with elements of trauma therapy allows my polymathic brain to witness a novel approach to life events interpretation. All of this let me understand the magic of what is possible regarding the alternation of human perception.

Many types of interventions could change our perception, be it multisensory AI virtual reality, near-death experiences, plant medicine travels, or the experience of surviving a severe physical illness. People have reported that after these events, a change in their perception transformed their life thereafter to such an extent that they felt as though they were privy to a miracle of love, starting a life of service, and enjoying the reality of every day. However, it is not the experience itself that changes perception. A switch of emotional engagement, which happens during such an experience, has changed the life of many. The next question is: If our imagination is akin to a virtual reality that we can access to change our emotional states and perception, do we need any stressful events or technology to enhance our lives?

Dear reader, your emotions are your treasure, an innate gift that leads to emotional engagements and lets you flourish with even more sensitivity without a glimpse of vulnerability. Being sensitive allows you to feel others, nature, and yourself with all subtle, tiny nuances. The same ability to share those feelings or empathy connects you with creativity, intuition, and higher blissful states, requiring emotional non-attachment or liberation, which will become a new norm soon.

We are all born sensitive; I never meet any human without the ability to feel. However, most of us are frozen or disconnected, emotionally stultified. Others are vulnerable and wounded and prefer not to touch the emotional zone, which is often a source of pain. Therefore, many of us prefer a life of self-control instead of the life of freedom. However, tidal waves of past emotional baggage could be processed, allowing you to enter the fresh waters of emotional health. Once you shift your perception from the outcome of your experiences and learning towards emotional processing and feeling, you will be granted access to your dormant emotive capability. Psychology states that the conscious mind doesn't manage our life, so why change our nature, trying to control it more and more instead of returning to our dormant emotional power and relaxing?

I invite you to enter a story that is not about rituals, discipline, or hard work. It is also not about persistence, which rewards 'one day.' I don't offer a receipt of the good life ever, as this is very individual. This book is my offer to open hearts and minds, written to lay a foundation and initiate a discussion about the 'world of senses,' sensitivity, and the dormant power of human emotions, which we need in the era of technology dominance. I invite you to become living evidence of true human potential. In trusting of your own nature, you will realize we are not destined to confront our emotions, and I hope my personal journey to discover this fact will serve as an inspiration.

# Foreword

Empathy is what human beings do. It is an evolved mechanism that is a fundamental part of our social nature. We live together, work together, and love together. Empathy has a physical signature in the brain, it is measurable physiologically. This physiologic signature varies substantially across individuals and like all traits, this has benefits and costs. In this volume, Elena Amber identifies the benefits of being an empath, as well as some of its downsides. Her honest discussion of her early family experiences, the emotional traumas she faced, and how these likely influenced her emotional sensitivity is quite revealing.

Empaths typically find themselves in service roles. Teachers, coaches, nurses, doctors, and many more professions attract empaths because these jobs help others to flourish. As Elena discusses, empaths are not only attracted to these professions, but they tend to excel in them because of their innate gifts. The ability to be fully immersed in people and what they are doing is important and valuable.

Nevertheless, there are costs to being highly sensitive. Chief among these is emotional contagion. Empaths suffer when others suffer, even when they see others at a distance. They cry at movies, they cry when seeing a lost dog, and they carry emotional pain longer than others do. Empaths, compared to others, are also more likely to be highly sensitive to non-emotional stimuli, often becoming motion-sick and suffering from migraines. As a result, they tend to be risk-averse and this can manifest as being standoffish.

Yet, when groups congregate, having even one highly sensitive person increases the group's effectiveness. Humans thrive on collective action and sensitive people like being part of a group and will work to make the group successful. The empath's social nature guides others on improving health and happiness. There are four primary factors that one can directly influence to improve the quality of life: sleep, exercise, diet, and the quality of social relationships. Highly sensitive people tend to be social givers. As a result, they typically have more friends and better relationships with family. This extends their healthspan.

For those of us who are less sensitive, there are lessons to be learned from the highly sensitive. First, give to get. The neural signature of social connection is indexed by the brain's release of the neurochemical oxytocin. Highly sensitive people release more oxytocin during social experiences than do others. The oxytocin-driven social connection system is, like other brain systems, adaptive. The more we give to others, the more they will reciprocate, increasing the brain's release of oxytocin. In this way, we can become not only more sensitive to others' needs, but we can improve the quality of our social relationships.

Second, people are inconsistent. Oxytocin, the neuro-chemical basis for social sensitivity, is inhibited and promoted by many of the 200 other neurochemicals active in the brain. We should not, therefore, expect even our closest friends, romantic partners, and family to engage with us the same way every time we encounter them. These neurochemical interactions occur outside of conscious awareness so emotionally healthy individuals need to be tolerant and accepting of others' quirkiness (and they of ours). These approaches to developing a rich social life are what make our time on this planet valuable. In a word, it is love.

**Dr. Paul J. Zak**, Professor, speaker, neuroeconomist, and author of *Immersion: The Science of the Extraordinary and the Source of Happiness*

# Chapter 1

# Life in Dreams

*People often create and believe their dreams, but the reality could be very different – mine was a disaster*

## Escape to a world of books which was full of dreams and miracles

It is so good to begin your morning waking up to the smell of homemade apple pie. You hear the chime of cups and spoons that seem to be talking to each other, preparing for the most important event of the morning. The sun is already shimmering in the red leaves, warming the earth with a soft autumn light and curling its rays into thin streams through the breeze that lifts the leaves and plays with them in flight. The birds are already chatting anxiously, and the bee says 'see you soon' to everyone because she is preparing to sleep all winter. The room is still in its morning dream, opening the flowers of the curtains, preparing for a beautiful day, as if everything is coming together to let you know: it will happen today!

My world was full of these wonders, full of adventures, brave heroes, and justice. In this world, good always won, and a tender heart knew no barriers. The stories of all the countries of the world had crossed the threshold of my room.

How many books had I read? I do not remember, but one day the school librarian looked at me sternly and said that I had gone through all the books that were suitable for my age, and she had nothing more to offer me. It is impossible to describe the feeling of dread I experienced at this – I could not imagine myself without books. They were my world and my shelter. Through them and in the world they provided for me, I could become anyone, meet anybody, find myself in the most unexpected places, and feel connected to everything around me. This world was known and familiar to me. I understood how the laws of the universe worked there and grew up with them as my support. I felt accepted and loved there, my friends were waiting for me, and there was my life.

It is not so rare for people to create worlds and escape into their beautiful dreams full of miracles. The reality, however, is often different. Mine was a disaster.

## The truth is I was living in the unfolding tragedy and drama

I barely remember my childhood. Memory was gently wiped away as if with a rubber eraser: a few episodes, several messages, and an abyss of darkness. The air of my real home was thick with tragedy, and life took place in dark violet hues, riddled with the pink scars of freshly healed newly obtained wounds. I was born diagnosed with rickets and a weak immune response, experiencing all sorts of diseases, including pneumonia. Winters were long in the place of my birth, so for six months every year, it was difficult to encounter sunshine. I was emotionally wounded, physically weak, vulnerable, and so sensitive that people said, 'she has no skin.' The words of others seeped into me, into my blood, and there was no protective barrier to prevent this.

I believed that the opinions of others were the only truth hurting me so much. It sounded logical to me when I was told the story that my birth was by a method which would be prohibited a year later and deemed 'inhumane.' The technique in question forced the child to be squeezed out of the mother using sheets folded into tight bundles. It seemed that I was not the one who wanted to be born, clutching at my small, safe world of the pregnant belly, where I was threatened by the outside world. The real world seemed so evil and harsh that we didn't fit together in any way, and there was no need to enter it.

In my youth, there was no smell of apple pies in our house, and I was one of those kids with the pre-planned role of becoming the glue in the disintegrating marriage. The drama of family betrayal was slowly unfolding, until my mother finally left us when I was six, pregnant with a third child that my father claimed could not possibly be his on the basis that there had been an absence of physical contact between them. My older sister was gravely different to me, including in her outward appearance, which was very provocative to the relatives on our father's side. My white curly hair, thin bones, light gray eyes, and higher grades in elementary school were an inexhaustible source of her anger, hatred, and desire to get rid of my presence. She had a petite body with straight black hair and dark brown eyes. My parents forced my sister to take responsibility for me as if she were my mother, and this was her nightmare. However, we were in the same boat because my father was diagnosed with a brain tumor, and we only really had each other. I understand why she escaped from home at the first opportunity, almost immediately after her course at the seamstress's college. It was a heavy burden to bear at such a young age: a younger sister and a father with an irreversible health problem.

I remember my horror at the first epileptic seizure, which I saw at age five, and even more a year later. Father's situation, condemned to live with a brain tumor and abandoned with two daughters, was not easy. Everyone talks about the plight of women and the wounded femininity of our times. This particular story is about a man who a woman used. The wound of a man, especially an intelligent and sensitive man, remains hidden so no one sees it. It is so deep that we will be processing this layer for centuries ahead.

The world around me seemed harsh because it was full of people and situations that I could neither accept nor change. Life also prevented me from helping the only person dear to me – my father. I waited all my life to kindle a connection with him, but my father was of Nordic blood, and the drama of his life froze his heart to the point where it was as cold and hard as an iceberg.

When someone close to us suffers, our own condition does not matter much. While surviving my childhood, I was developing sensitivity to the point where I knew in advance whether my father's blood pressure would change that day, or if there were any changes in his nighttime breathing, which I could feel through a couple of walls. Most prominent in my mind was the notion that he would need my help, that I would be unable to oblige, and that this would render me on my own. However, it seems I had the resources to deal with that situation, as my inner strength had awoken in a strange instance earlier in my life.

I had been hit by a car, severely, and the driver had fled the scene. I remember the car moving, running within millimeters of it, crossing the street. It collided with my left hip, I ricocheted off the chassis, and fell to the side of the road after arcing through the air. 'So, this is it, and I die?' was the thought in my head when I hit the asphalt. My last memory before losing consciousness was the smell of green grass on the soil, and then I switched off to reality. I didn't see any white tunnels of light, and no angels came to me with a message. Once I opened my eyes, two people were present, trying to help me. I remember the following scenes as though they were excerpts from a film: the deepness of my left leg wound, the taste of blood on my lips, the feminine voice saying 'take out our bus' to her husband, the smell of iodine, and the roughness of freshly applied bandages. I understood that the bus that belonged to this pair was too close to the pedestrian crossing, and was covering the road's view to pedestrians, which was what had caused my incident. They had used medicine on my leg, but everything else had been untouched, as if nothing had really happened. I sat down, then stood, then told those people, 'I am okay,' and walked away from the place. I was less than seven years old.

I believe that was a moment when my spirit walked into my life, initiating my strength. I can't even imagine letting a child of such a tender age go home alone after such a shocking episode. Could you? Nevertheless, my condition was not severe, and I had the power to convince adults. Many years later, when I was granted a chance to reconnect with my mother again, we spent a few weeks together after a break of 35 years. I asked her about this episode, but she could not recall it.

## There are always teachers, preachers, and 'best friends' available

However, it took me a long time to fully connect with my inner power, and it was a journey. At first, I lost my hope for human kindness and the possibility of friendship. This began with my sister, who was always cheating me, and kidding me without me realizing it. It was as though I was in a cocoon that didn't let me see what people could be. I consistently and stupidly rejected the possibility of thinking badly about people. One day this fault in me was remedied, when our parents sent us to play out in the yard. The day was calm and warm, with nobody around. There was an old-modeled swing with a prominent crossbar and a base in the middle. It allowed children to sit on opposite sides of the crossbar and take turns swinging the swing, and my sister quickly took a side with comfortable handles for balance. The handles on my side were broken, but my sister told me to pick up a wooden stick and use it as the handle. I followed her instructions, since she was older and everyone older had authority over me. Of course, the stick leaning against the crossbar of the swing could not hold me while swinging, I fell on my left elbow, and it broke. That was when I realized that you probably should not believe everything everyone tells you.

My two friendship trials in elementary school ended in thefts after I invited the girls to play at home. One took the money openly left on the table, the other the family box with silver teaspoons. We had everything returned after I spoke to their parents and got everything back. It taught me how to protect myself, but it also made me wonder if people have good intentions and if 'best friends' are really that good. My belief that people are always generous and supportive of each other was finally obliterated when we met with my neighbor and childhood friend for a play. She took a charming chocolate bar from her pocket, opened it, and asked, 'Do you want chocolate?' 'Yes, indeed,' I said. 'Why don't you go and buy some' was the answer, and she ate alone in front of my eyes. It was a bad joke. My father barely had the money for bread and milk.

That was not the only moment I felt like I was being made into an outcast. In high school, I finally found a close soul who could draw extremely well and also respected books and poems. We started to spend every day together. One day she told me I could not come anymore because her mother said 'she overeats.' There was certainly truth to this statement because the food in their house was delicious, but I was also constantly hungry, as in my house we often only had potatoes. However, when somebody uses such raw truth without empathy, it can be deadly. It touched me to my very core, this notion of falling short of expectations. The idea that I was perceived in the same light as a beggar devastated me. Was I really that way? Was I responsible for my situation? I didn't think so, but I was ashamed of myself, feeling the abyss between the acceptance of 'normal people' and myself.

That was when I understood that people could be judged for their material status and not for who they are, one of the fundamental inequalities of modern society. My father raised me in a culture of sharing the last piece with others, but I realized that not everybody was like that.

Being not enough, I created authorities for myself, and allowed teachers to become my preachers. One of them told me every day to stay after school just to listen to her monologue about how I needed to be responsible and take care of myself because I did not have a mother. She explained that she deeply cared for me as a woman, and I began to put her on a pedestal, feeling that her patronizing was necessary for me to become qualified as a member of society. Another case occurred when we started algebra. I used to only to get As in math, but I began to have a lot of trouble with algebra as it didn't make sense to me. I eventually learned that math before algebra was sacred, and algebra turned us off from non-linear understanding and connection with nature, but that happened about 20 years later. Back at school, my new math teacher turned me into a whipping doll by commenting on me in every class. She publicly called me a negligent, inattentive, and arrogant pupil. She was kind enough to explain it to me one day, pointing out how I looked at her and what kind of expression I had on my face. Her issue was my particular style of looking at others with my chin up, which probably made me look dismissive. The reason for this was my strong astigmatism, but she did not know this and did not bother to understand.

## When everyone around you tells you that something is wrong with you, you finally believe it

When we disconnect from our core, believing in external reality takes a short time, and it may not be the best experience. People told me so many times that I was not good enough that I finally gave up on myself. Without positive feedback from the outside world, we tend to get sick like flowers that we don't water appropriately. Positive energy is like water for growing our self-esteem. If we don't find a source within, we build our identity on the external opinion and someone else's perception of us. This external opinion could be right, but there is just as much chance that it could be wrong. The fear of not being accepted is so intense that we tend to become like others at any price, so they don't see us as an outcast.

No one is better than another; therefore, in a warm society, it is normal to be associated with family and build a societal identity. In a harsh or cold environment, we must find another source within us and connect to it as an alternative. From a spiritual perspective, there are no fatherless or motherless people are in this world, and no one is abandoned, but this depends on which level we are looking for. When I finally understood this, I realized that people who find themselves in difficult life circumstances take an alternative path. They do not become strong by the support of others and do not depend on anyone. They usually shy away from associations with other humans and live a separate, single life. However, once they heal their hearts, they can become great leaders as they feel for others and have differentiated views on life. The lack of need for social connection does not make them unnecessary in the sense of belonging. However, they question it and get to where they truly belong at a faster pace.

I wish somebody could have explained all this to me as early as possible, but I didn't understand it in my teenage years. What I knew for sure was that I was different, alien, and therefore decided something was wrong with me. I could not accept the harshness of the world around me when others were suppressed, directed to false actions, or betrayed. My sense of justice was over-alerted; life was a threat, and I was full of fears and constantly needed to protect myself without support from anybody. I was not a victim anymore, yet I was like a soldier whose war had never ended. Ongoing anxiety led my body to react.

In addition to my severe astigmatism, I lost my sight almost to the point of blindness (−12, −14). Thus, my vision became very divided: most of the truth I could not see, and the others I saw only from a certain angle. Why did it happen so? I could not see the lies and cruelty around me, so I decided to stop seeing them. What could be better than to 'close my eyes to it,' i.e., become blind? The source of the most pain was a lie. I felt all the feelings and thoughts of everyone around me and could not understand why people still gathered at the same table if they hated each other, why they behaved as though in a theater play if they didn't love each other, and why people are so dishonest to each other. I couldn't imagine myself living that life. It was a nightmare for me to imagine that people would realize that I understood everything that was going on, and as soon as I realized they were on to me, I cut them from my life. Anxiety rose, and doctors offered me my first antidepressants (I was high school age). My only dream was to escape as quickly as possible, as I imagined the world was different 'out there.' The feeling of loneliness grew after every school day. My first full nighttime panic attack happened when I entered puberty.

Darkness had entered my soul, as it enters any sensitive person that does not allow themselves to fill with emotions or express them, simply because we hate the thought of harming others. Stuck between inner feelings and hatred of what we see, we are afraid of ourselves and suppress emotions because nothing could be worse than becoming 'one of them.' This situation is ideal for growth if one understands how polarities work, but I was still isolated from this knowledge.

I was over my dreams, hopes, failures, shame, guilt, and especially 'ways out' pointed out by teachers, preachers, and 'best friends' around me. In ecology, if we influence the ecosystem for a long enough time, it will absorb as many interventions as possible, but this will change its status by finding another point of status quo equilibrium. One day we will see a renewed, newborn system that has a completely new quality, which can be and do other things that were not even dreamed of before. Therefore, some people believe that evolution is a process of cumulative change, where once a particular characteristic is considered beneficial to life, anyone who develops it will survive better. I believe in incremental change, but when its cumulative volume changes the entire system, it is like a breakthrough. My life system reached this bifurcation point, after which my system could never be the same again. Therefore, my understanding of evolution is a chain of such bifurcation points, which could be natural, cumulative, or forced and spontaneous. That was my first change of personality.

Some people believe in multiple lives within one. Do you? I think we change our life every time we drastically change our personalities. It happens when we go through dark nights of the soul, which is the death of the current personality. Each time we change our very skin of who we believe we are, we begin a new life. The change is confirmed by new people around us, relocations or long travels, new marriages, new unknown qualities of ourselves, new tastes, new jobs, new appearances, and so on. Ask anyone how they know that a new life has begun. Everything mentioned will be in the aforementioned description, but most importantly, the change in the inner world state. We know that we become entirely different, and such is our life. Would you not call it rebirth to a new life? I finally realized that my decision to close my eyes to all this harshness and detachment from my feelings did not work. I understood that everyone around me was doing what they were, yet I was no different because I was also causing damage – but in my case, the damage was to no one but myself.

## What is a high sensitivity, and who are sensitives?

In your scientific search, you will find that, according to the environmental sensitivity theory, people differ in their ability to perceive and process information about their environment due to neurobiological differences in their brains, which genetic differences partly explain. While this means that sensitivity has a genetic basis, studies have shown that it is equally dependent on people's environment and life experiences.

Environments of any kind affect highly sensitive people more than others, whether just the physical world outside or the social realm. Scientists believe this is so because we develop sensitivity as a survival tool that helps us predict threats earlier and adapt better. Highly sensitive people experience both sides of emotions, pain and pleasure. I believe that the term 'highly sensitive person' was first used in work related to the sensory processing sensitivity of Dr. Elaine Aron, who points out that there are about 15–20% of highly sensitive people in the world. Later, other scientists' works showed that any other species, such as dogs, fish, and birds, can also have this quality.

Sensitives have a dedication to fairness and justice, valuing others. They also tend to demonstrate unusual perspectives, a different vision, and a way of thinking that others call 'innovative.' Increased perception and deeper processing let sensitive people see things differently. They do not act immediately, as they need more time to process more information and tend to be more cautious. Sensitives are well aware of the attitudes and feelings of other people, as they have a high sense of empathy. They know the subtleties of the environment and easily 'read between the lines' in a situation.

Scientists say that the environment affects sensitive people the most. They could be the best creatives, artists, advisors, trainers, and curious scientists in a warm social atmosphere. A cold environment could make sensitives super-resistant and stubborn; rebels are also born here. Under the influence of negative experiences, such as stressful life or childhood without family care, sensitive people become hardened and freeze their ability to be sensitive. However, we must remember that if we do not feel pain, we cannot feel joy; I will discuss this phenomenon later in the book.

A few more details are needed. Sensitivity is equally manifest in both men and women, with the only difference being that girls are typically allowed to be more sensitive. Boys are often forbidden to the point of severe punishment because their sensitivity is considered the worst male social quality. There are also introverts and extroverts with high sensitivity, and both are affected, although there are more introverts. It could also be that introverts are not punished for being sensitive; society seems to accept them. Extroverts must have a hard time with sensitivity simply because their environment is more dynamic, so they must deplete more often. I have personally been on both sides as an intro and extrovert at different periods of my life. It seems we could swap these qualities.

To feel more than others is a heavy burden. When others lie, and you cannot tell anybody, it is as if they are whispering behind your back, and you cannot react. They allow themselves to punish others, but you cannot do anything about this situation. We feel pain, and sensitives often find themselves feeling guilty for not being able to help or ashamed of the behavior of others as if it were their own. It is hard to feel useless for not being able to help your loved ones with their health or broken lives and feeling responsible for them. My mind became a machine, racing 24 hours a day, anticipating the next threat available with the task of protecting myself and my father.

## I survived, but life became an everyday challenge

Further pressure pushed me to find a way to cope with life. Probably this pressure caused my bifurcation, where two of my worlds suddenly merged into one: I began to see book characters in real people. This changed everything for me in ways I struggled to believe. I suddenly realized that this world is no different from the ones with which I am so familiar from my books. I didn't notice it before because I could only look from one point of view, use one angle, and look at everyday life from one corner. Maybe I came out of that corner, unable to sit there anymore, but it was more likely that newly emerged feeling that I experienced. Once I experienced the world as one which I was already familiar with, my confidence was born.

When we gain confidence, we increase our energy level and thus can be more open to reality. It is also true that confidence conquers fear, so there are two ways to do psychological work. One is to focus on therapy and deal with fears. Another, completely different, is to build confidence by coaching. It is well accepted that when a person acquires at least one source of confidence, they can cope much better with life's circumstances. I recently heard a true story about a doctor who has helped so many with childhood dyslexia by finding one source, one activity, and one subject of interest that brings confidence to that child with the support of teachers and parents. It has been observed that kids can easily handle a broader range of other activities once their confidence grows. My father was an herbalist, so biology became my first passion and winning at Olympiads and regional competitions supported my faith. Soon after, I could even ask a school for a small job of classroom cleaning, so I found my way to pocket money.

Not all cases could be sorted out this way, at least in my personal experience, but confidence primarily neutralizes our fears. Thus, seeing a polarity and concentrating on the second pole brings us relief and the ability to move forward. Sages have practiced the polarity neutralization method for centuries, and it is described in many practices, including hermetic traditions. Hermetic practitioners also admitted someone's ability to understand the polarity principle alone, without being involved in any specific teachings, just from life experience. I wish everyone could be familiar with the polarity principle and successfully practice it.

The energy level provided by confidence allowed me to see life differently and deepened my understanding of human nature and behavior. I still observed harshness and inappropriate behavior, but I started to see why people do that. What a gift it is to understand others! The ability to understand and therefore predict the behavior of others allows us to create larger communities, overcoming closed groups and tribalism. Understanding the behavior of others also gives us the ability to predict not only individual but public and social situations, so we can more easily build social bonds without fear of being threatened by others.

The effect of this merge, when two of my worlds united, was of great importance. First, I understood that the pain I experienced was self-created because I only wanted the world to be my way. I didn't accept it, didn't try to understand it, didn't manage it by focusing on the small and good things, didn't value others being vulnerable without the ability to trust, and wished everyone would become my healers. I was like a victim but was able to reflect on this part, so my victimhood died. What dies is not us but our personality and the created image, a part of our ego, ideas, and perceptions of who we are. The hero of my imaginary life drama, the girl, was immediately reborn as a phoenix. She realized that she could be the one who could deal with all of life's characters because she understood them and could predict their behavior. Another beautiful thing happens when we become confident with others: we build new social connections and identify 'our people.'

The most impactful aspect of polarity work, connected with an inner change of our quality, I called 'the grand finale,' the end of the scenario we play out in our life situation. Once we have changed, we no longer play the same roles and do not belong to old scenarios. Psychologist Eric Berne described quite a few games that people play, which is a fantastic illustration of life's theater. I observe that games are not very different, and the number of variations is quite limited. For a moment, I realized that I was no longer afraid and no longer waiting for anyone. Instead, I was able to get out of my corner of life and communicate with people directly.

It was a critical moment in my life, as confidence allowed me to build a different personality by choosing a distinct identity. I name personalities 'avatars,' and I already knew from reading many learned people on the subject that we can change personalities. A breakthrough happened when I realized that this ability exists within us in this lifetime. When I was experiencing the process of changing personality, I saw the image evoked by the children's cartoon character Kaa the python, a friend of the brave Mowgli, a jungle boy raised by wolves. I can feel the python's words, 'it's hard to change a skin,' in the scene that shows him during the spring molt that snakes go through every year. We all build or change avatars to survive in difficult situations. However, we tend to associate ourselves with our personalities, identifying ourselves with one role, which is a considerable limitation. Changing skin, therefore, is very difficult.

We build our personalities around core expectations, and they are interconnected. Once we achieve the expectation (or crush it), the old personality doesn't serve us anymore. Did you face situations when after a significant win (or failure), you didn't know who you were, where you should go, and what to do next, and you ended up getting lost? Steadily you could build a new personality, but usually, it takes time. We tend to spend so much time changing our expectations for reality. Life is a process of change. The sooner we accept it, the smoother the process of building expectations will be; we need to carefully listen to life to know which quality we need to release or obtain. Happy are those who are privileged with faith in the life process, so wise men accept it all.

As soon as we no longer need them, the scenarios would end, and all the characters from the completed scenarios disappear from our lives just because we don't need them anymore. If we play several games with the same person and don't mean to separate from them yet, their behavior towards us will suddenly change, so they will become a completely new person to us. Our new identity will show up to others also. Thus, my second life, my dark period of rebellion, had begun.

# Chapter 2

# Reason

*Each of us is here for a reason,*
*but they forgot to write mine*

## Finally, I got it and understood how to thrive in this harsh world

By the end of high school, it became effortless for me to recognize what people thought, how they would react and behave, and how to drive their emotions in a different direction. For example, how to avoid anger releases which are so dangerous for others. I could somehow feel what would be appropriate to say, how to act, and how to change tensions in the room's atmosphere. However, I also understood what to do if I needed something. Do you know the meaning of manipulation? Sensitives have all the abilities to become great manipulators based on the fact they feel what others need. Can you imagine what one could get from the other if they knew which button to press? Manipulation is the ability to get what you want at the expense of others in a way that makes them want to do it for you. It is challenge number one, which any sensitive would face in developing their abilities. As with any other action, manipulation has a reaction and consequences. Therefore, it is essential to recognize what is good and bad when you can feel more about other people.

Good intentions could become a direct path to darkness. Sensitives, who usually don't harm others, could step into manipulation in two ways. One is through being a service to others when we step in to manipulation as pleasers to others. Pleasing is 'do-goodery' or service for others with unconscious motives to get attention, acceptance, or esteem for an exchange. There is nothing good or bad in the exchange itself per se; for example, communication is a process of exchange. However, if it is not declared, it becomes the covert wish of someone for another to behave in a particular way, which is manipulation. Ask yourself if it hurts you if someone doesn't act as you wish despite you doing so much for them. A healthy understanding is that 'being needed is not being loved.' All we need is love, but it cannot be at the price of pleasing others. True love and acceptance start within us. If it is in place, the world will reflect it on you and never the other way around. If others don't accept you, you have work to do and accept yourself without providing for them first. You cannot be good only if you do certain things. This is the absence of love towards yourself, your starting point to get out of this game.

Another challenge to the power of sensitivity is the tendency to defend others when we step into a manipulation game as rescuers. It happened to me when a new girl joined our class. She was from a needy family, wore make-up beyond the social norms, was very aggressive towards others, and generally received the worst grades. Indeed, she soon became the center of ostracism, and I became her rescuer. Sensitive people cannot see if someone is being punished in front of their eyes if someone needs a defense. Protecting others, we are not always able to recognize the game. Therefore, it is easy to use or manipulate sensitive people. Show sensitives injustice, and they will jump into the role of hero. The truth is that sensitive people see themselves in every victim and cannot let that happen. Most of the time, we don't understand that inner work needs to be done, but we start to 'do the work' in the outer world and protect those who need to go through the test themselves. Sometimes we can become so arrogant that we believe we have the right to suppress offenders, harshly using the flag of justice as our reason. Rebellion is helpful, but it has its borders.

I remember how the Buddhist view of life was complex for me to understand because I could not grasp how the world could already be perfect if there is so much pain and injustice. I did not know yet that this was not all the world amounted to. It was 'my world' because each of us plays out our tragedy and our triumph personally – the fabric of life based on our perception. We look through our lenses so that each of us has a different experience in the same situation. It is also true that life reflects our internal emotional state, which means you could consider it an attractor of our experience. We have attracted some situations with possible tangible explanations, but some seem to be destined. Whether you believe we create an experience or not, or if there is a direct responsibility of the individual for them, it doesn't matter. Although we may not be responsible for our life situations, we are fully responsible for how quickly we move out from those we don't like and our emotional aftertaste. I understand that they are all designed as pure potential. We have equal chances to transform them into a thread or an opportunity.

Back at my school, however, I could not grasp the meaning that everyone has their own agenda, even if we are in the same boat. That means we have a personal responsibility to become strong. A sensitive person who has built up muscles forgets about this boundary too often. If a weak point still needs to be healed, others become a reminder of this weakness in such a way that the dimension of existing trauma overflows, following emotional triggers. Everything would be balanced if we could intervene in violence and humiliation without becoming a tyrant. We should not lose sight of this. But if a person is in their negative pole, that means that they play the other side of a victim and become a tyrant who is still an enslaved person just acting in revenge.

The main characteristic of tyrants is the belief that they can decide what to do with others to get what they want, and this is a direct path for sensitives to step in to manipulation. Having become real cynics of human motives, we might think that we can do whatever we want to protect weakness, entirely irrespective of the path of another. Superiority means inequality; however, we must remain human under all circumstances. The judgment that someone is wrong comes from an inability to see the big picture and our shadows. When we start to protect others with the slogan 'we are good, they are bad,' we are stepping on a slippery margin. Thus, the rebel becomes arrogant towards others, thinking they have the right to be so because others are worse. However, it was a very dark period in my life when I learned how we create the causes of a 'hard life' and what an open heart means.

It was my negative pole of sensitivity. Most of those who achieve it become aggressive, burly, careless, and rigid personalities. Protecting others requires a clear inner vision of what is happening and the strength to keep the light in our hearts. Life is a class where everyone has the opportunity to graduate with honors, and it is not we who decide what role one should play. Our best ability is to see the truth and know that everyone has enough strength. Our strength is to stay who we really are.

## The focus of attention on others disconnected me from myself

Playing a rescuer role, I was deeply in survival mode, which completely disconnected me from myself. Constant focus on public and social situations, anticipating the following thread, took 100% of my attention. I was caught up in the film scenario of my perception, completely losing myself.

I could easily explain what others wanted or felt, but I could not answer any questions about myself. I had no hobbies or extracurricular music or art classes like other pupils. Nothing caught my attention, nothing was interesting, and biology was forgotten as a childish interest that a worrier should not have. At my college age, when it came time to decide which faculty to choose for the University, I barely knew what I liked. I had no interest in anything or anyone, couldn't answer the simple question 'What do you want?' and had no desires. Please understand me right; I wanted to eat or sleep or do something, but what I am trying to explain here is that nothing held my long-term attention. My emotional engagement connects me to sadness, pain, or anger as an exception. These emotions reflect the absence of individual psychological safety, which we desperately need in order to open the door to the learning curiosity level. This door of my inner world was closed. I thought I understood the whole world but lost my North Star. Feelings of worthlessness, lack of talent to perform at the annual school events, and loss of purpose increased self-guilt and shame. I had no idea why I was there and where I needed to go. A sage would have congratulated me on reaching this point of potential for bifurcation, but I had no such friend, and the stimuli of the outside world shuttered my listening channel.

When we are in survival mode, we only have energy for protection. It may even be an inspiring challenge and an increase in courage, but we cannot experience survival for a long time; it is very tiring. Survival is an excellent condition, necessary in an actual situation, but the phrase 'warriors need to return from the war' is appropriate. My rebellious avatar was courageous, but fatigue cut off her life interest because survival and curiosity are incompatible. Therefore, we need to ensure we are safe enough to experience the other end of the emotional spectrum, and indeed, we need to stop trying so hard to survive if there's no actual threat. Each emotional level has its energy; the funnel of traumatic reactions goes down the emotional scale. Thus, rebellion is better than neglect: when a dying kitten starts biting you, it means it is willing to take a life. Yet if it doesn't want to protect itself, being indifferent to food seriously indicates the possibility of the coming end. Rebellion is aggression; it has more energy, which is already a good sign. It is a step above indifference. People often think that fear is the opposite of love, but this is not so – fear is the opposite of courage. Love's opposite pole is indifference, and I was very close to it.

Later on, when I read the life story of Freud, I had a eureka moment of understanding about what exactly caused my constant sadness, which was a loss of belonging. I paid serious attention to the fact that Freud experienced the same situation with sciences, where he could not find the one to belong. Sense of belonging is vitally essential for us, and it doesn't matter if we belong to the social domain – such as family, community, society, or country –or the natural domain – forests, rivers, or friends from other species such as cats, dogs, or stars of the Universe. We need to belong somewhere. Freud found an elegant solution to his situation by starting a new discipline called 'psychology,' failing to find the one that could best accommodate his knowledge. Thus, he pointed out that if we could not find where to belong, it could be a situation where we could start something by ourselves. In other words, if we don't feel at home anywhere, we might need to build one. If we don't feel right with any community members, we may need to start our own community. This excellent lesson is a guiding light in the dark times of the shutdown. My case was even simpler, as being a polymath, I was meant to be ignited by connections, intersections and interdisciplinary views for existing fields. However, dominated by the educational and societal approach of 'specialization,' I was misled about existing opportunities.

I was at a crossroads because my rebel avatar ended up in a group of classmates when someone offered me a needle and syringe. I realized that they all had a dose. The small town where we lived was once known as a city of thieves and drug addicts. We already had a few being treated with the first overdose treatments, and it was clear that this was not the world where I belonged. It only took me a few seconds to leave, saying a firm 'no' to the proposal, realizing that any system would fight for its member, and I reached the point of 'no return.' It was time for a clear decision.

### We could feel threats the same way we feel opportunities, it is a matter of where we choose to focus our attention

Have you ever felt that you are meant for more? I have had an exciting experience with such a feeling. In my case, because I never knew what I was made for, I didn't know what I needed to do or where to go. However, I knew whether this was my lot or not. Later, I learned that we could have a beautiful extension of that feeling if we do not insist on knowing for sure before taking action from our side. Once explored, it made my search for opportunities much more straightforward. How does it work? If I feel 'this is not my lot' (I am meant for more), I only need to shut a door to what I don't like for a new opportunity to arrive. One might think this is easy, but I would not support such a conclusion because it is difficult to say 'no' and leave what you have already arranged. Imagine if this is a comfortable payroll, a beautiful house, or established relationships where you don't feel happy. It is challenging to leave three things: our expectations, our built personality, and the time we invest. Yet, once we only start to close the old door will a new door to opportunity simultaneously begin to open. It is fascinating to experience this construction of life simply knowing it exists. I gave it the name 'law of flow,' meaning we need to organize a space or give up on something to receive something new. I gave up my rescuer personality and the idea I needed to make the world a better place by being Robin Hood.

Termination of my rebellion path worked! I immediately got to feel what it is to become a young entrepreneur, and my older friend helped me in this process. Like many entrepreneurs, I forewent my university education to treat people, their needs, and desires. The business turned out to be a simple process of linking a customer's problems and their solutions. I found entrepreneurs to be bold, flamboyant, self-responsible, and self-confident. In fact, at 17, I could provide for myself and significantly contribute to the entire family of my newly married sister and her newborn while her partner was in professional retraining. Life consists of waves, and if we make the right choices, it gives us opportunities. I think I made the right choice. I also learned that it's much better to experience sadness when the table is full, the shoes are warm enough, and there is someone to talk to. Life teaches me this rule number one: 'arrange your basics,' or take ultimate responsibility for yourself. Responsibility is a very interesting pole, and it balances power. Once we take responsibility for our life, we have the power to change it in any direction. Likewise, once we have power, we must take responsibility. Otherwise, it will steadily destroy us and everything we create. Do you ever ask the question, why is a power given? It is an interesting perspective if you are fascinated by cycles like I am. History cycles show so many samples of the 'power–responsibility' polarity harmonization, where any mighty

Empire which doesn't care about the world around serves as a perfect sample. The absence of responsibility always follows the Empire's power destruction. Taking individual responsibility for our life raises our inner power; we call it confidence. Any time we raise such a power, we have new opportunities for its realization on the horizon.

Coming back to basics, they cannot replace your North Star, but they make life easier and, more importantly, give you the necessary level of psychological safety and security. I consider individual psychological safety as the base confidence which opens a whole range of opportunities for us, including the possibility of leaving survival mode by accessing the mode of creation. Once this happens, life becomes much more enjoyable than just making money, and any duty suddenly feels like a gift.

The spark of such a development was bound to open the understanding of the law of attraction for me. The way I learned the feeling of individual psychological safety was mundane, through arranging my life basics. However, once I experienced how to feel safe, I got to know this emotion, and I could find a way to experience it again without arranging material comfort first. Some people achieve safety by putting life around them, but some evaluate how to get there through a shortcut of meditation or deep emotional engagement. Once we set up that feeling within, outside life is arranged by itself, becoming the reflection of our inner state. How it works is fascinating, and I found two categories of people who have already established access to it: spiritual practitioners and entrepreneurs. I understand you may think about such a combination as a crazy idea, but later in the book, I will share how I was able to prove it through my Master's thesis research.

Coming back to the sense of life. If you feel you are meant for more, you need to search for what is yours, so start it and never give up. Do what you do, but wait for messengers. Who are they, and who could be your messenger? Life speaks to us through people and through books, films, and situations. Mine speaks to me very often through information retrieval. I don't know how, but I can find the most fantastic information if I turn off logic and trust the process of searching. Life is simply a flow of information, and the part you need is looking for you as much as you are looking for it. You have already dedicated yourself to each other.

My experience with life messages is also hilarious. I remember one day I was so mad at my friend and went outside to catch a coach, when suddenly, through the veil of my thoughts, I heard the following phrase loudly right to my ears: 'I am not going to take it!' I was so shocked that I stopped and looked around, lonely on the street in the earlier hours of the day, with only one figure walking up there, wrapped in a coat. Maybe she said that, as people often talk loudly to themselves if they are experiencing a strong emotional feeling. Perhaps it was just a voice in my head, I still don't know, but I know for sure what appeared on my face, and it was a broad smile. I understood this message was addressing me.

Another time, I was in the middle of an emotional episode. Still, I needed to finish a business meeting before I could connect to myself and put it in order, so I sat on a bench in front of the business center and waited 15 minutes to come in. A young girl passed by and suddenly turned to me, asking, 'are you, Elena?' 'Yes,' I said, thinking that she was the secretary they sent to meet me (what a strange idea). I asked if she was a secretary, but she was not the woman I was supposed to meet. I asked her name, and she said, smiling, 'my name is Vera.' Vera is the name whose direct translation means 'faith.' The lady left. I was sitting on that bench, utterly discouraged because I suddenly had that 'message feeling' again. Faith was a word of encouragement that I needed at this exact moment. I smiled broadly. I wrote this paragraph specifically for those who believe in messages and those who have never received them.

If you look at life waiting for a message, such a minor detail to appear during emotionally charged episodes, broadening your focus rather than being absorbed by drama, you will get them. The only requirement is to be prepared, just like in a movie, taking the third position of the observer. This position allows us to get life messages, recover faster, and find more hidden meaning in every second of our lives. I call this ability 'reading between the lines,' where we get the essence of what is going on, shifting attention to information rather than concentrating on the experience details or people involved.

I got my message from the same friend who loved to eat chocolate alone in front of another who unexpectedly came to my house and shared her dream. She told me she was leaving town in three weeks to go to university because she wanted to study mathematics. The conversation was bright; she was on top and shone like never before. The adventure was in her voice, and she was so connected and enlightening in her speech that I forgot every bad second between us. She was a stream of new potential in her own right. 'Do they have a psychology department?' I asked. They didn't, but there was an opportunity to specialize in it as a biology or history student. Such a surprise, I had a few certificates and wins from biology Olympiads and regional competitions. Once I realized that, my heart started beating so fast that I couldn't stop it. My hands were getting wet; I was so worried but happy at the same time; I felt it was a call when she told me: 'Let's go together to a big city, it will be easier for the two of us.'

Whether it was her mother who wisely sent her to me, my dad had a hand in it, or she was afraid to go alone, I have no idea, and I don't think it really matters. The important thing is that if you feel you are meant for more, you should never give up. I felt uplifted, but at the same time, I was scared to death. First, it was a whole gap year after school, and my recent marks had been a disaster. My high school diploma mostly had just satisfactory grades and an unsatisfactory behavior mark due to my rebellious actions. Yet I had no doubts about my life message!

The opportunity to finally leave this town became a bright ember that ignited my childhood dreams, making them radiant. University and the big city! I'm sure this friend was the messenger, but I could only get the message because my heart no longer held on to the teenage episode between us. I was free from any resentment, being thankful for what I had. A week later, we were both sitting in an intercity bus driving us to an unknown future.

My task was to pass three exams, biology being the main one, and I had only two weeks to prepare. What a time it was.

We were arranged on the University campus in a room with four or five other girls from different faculties. Everybody studied day and night, forgetting to eat or walk out for fresh air. There were so many new things around, but the atmosphere was electric with somebody's drama of a failed exam or somebody's ecstasy at being accepted. My brain could remember tons of information about my interests, and I crammed stuff in like crazy.

I remember the night before the exam. Importance was at the highest because a good mark meant I could take two other exams and be considered a candidate. I opened my biology textbook, looked at the material which was on crayfish, read it through once again, and put a same-page book under my pillow. In the morning, I was nervous. The University auditorium was packed as the faculty was popular. I pulled out the exam questions and saw a question about cancer – namely, a simple crayfish and its structure from the field of zoology. In a particular order from the book, I remembered all its identification of parts and their functions; the material was from a page I opened yesterday. More specifically, I remembered this part of the textbook – not just precisely, but verbatim. The other two questions weren't as good; one was from botany, which I barely remembered. My time came, and I sat down, starting my answer from a weaker question. The teacher was the chairwoman of the panel, she was a nerd, and in a second, I realized that I would not pass. I asked her for a pause, referring to the necessity to concentrate, and got the opportunity. I sat at the desk and realized I would not remember anything else. The beating of my heart slowed, I began to fall from panic into the funnel of the collapse of my hope, and suddenly something happened.

My eye caught a modest woman sitting on the edge of the magnificent chairwoman of the table and a badge that read, 'department of zoology.' That was my golden ticket, my crayfish! As soon as the previous candidate stood up, I rushed to the chair in front of her and began to tell her everything I knew about it. She stopped me, but I said that's not all. She said that was enough, but I insisted that I found arthropods beautiful and that they were unique to me. Then I saw her clear handwriting put some notes in my documents, and she stood up.

Imagine a vast old-fashioned university auditorium descending to a podium filled with several hundred candidates, building up the logic of answering exam questions so diligently that the dust of summer air trembles with tension in the transparent sunlight. 'Audience, be quiet!' Her loud voice stopped the whole process. 'Stand up,' she said, and cottony legs lifted me. All eyes were on me, and it was the worst moment of my life. I wore glasses and was very shy. On top of that, I had accidentally broken part of my glasses in the university's bustle, so the central axis tilted strongly to the right, crossed by a large fissure. To answer questions, however, I put them on because, without glasses, I saw only colored blurry spots; my vision was lost in childhood. And now everyone saw me, my glasses, my face red out of tension, and heard her unbelievable words, culminating the psychological drama of my ugly duckling. 'Candidates! I want to introduce a student who has the potential to become a pride of our faculty, and I want us all to wish her well now.' She probably was from another culture, as I could not even imagine being noticed in front of the others; I felt so uncom-fortable thinking about how they now felt about themselves.

I was accepted.

In that moment, my sensitive girl personality, biology certificates, chocolate friend, entrepreneurship for raising my level of confidence, mysterious book page with cancer, ability to sense a moment of opportunity – all of that became a logical chain of life's events, showing the reason. I was not forgotten at all; I went through preparations for a significant role in my life.

What was new for me was the experience of meeting a person who was deeply involved in my life, although I didn't know her. That was the first time I met one of the people I call 'angels,' and there were few such meetings in my life. Such encounters always give us enormous support and sudden changes for the good in our life direction. This day I understood that sensitive people could feel threats the same way as they could feel opportunities, the matter of our attention focus. Another idea became so vivid after being able to follow breadcrumbs, such as information in the textbook coinciding with the question I was supposed to answer and the examiner faculty sign. Precisely, when such synchronicity happens, we suddenly reveal waves of 'cause-and-effect' connections and feel the presence of a bigger plan than we could see ourselves.

## Escape for the new life when I left home, and all the old stories left behind

I was shown a glimpse of the possibility of becoming someone meaningful for the faculty, leaving home and all the heavy stories behind. I always dreamed of escape, so I jumped into that opportunity. It was enough to have just one person who believed in me.

Here I am, a new personality, in the world of equal opportunities from a Universe in her third life. Later, I realized that a former biology teacher of mine had a word with her university mate (my zoology faculty angel) about me. What were the chances that I would feel the need to hold my exam answer with that exact person, and that we would spontaneously connect without any arrangements? She was the 'right person.' Always follow such inner intentions, no matter how stupid your logical mind thinks they are; listen to your heart. One would call it a coincidence, but it's hard to believe, just because it all feels like a rehearsed episode from a movie. We don't need to know precisely how it works, but we need to listen to our heartbeat once we resonate with ideas, propositions, or opportunities because life sends signs and support for those who follow the path. Since then, a feeling of me 'being in a cinema episode' within a real-life context has become a clear sign that I follow through with something specifically arranged. This situation shows me that I follow the path aligned. It took a while to get used to such episodes; however, I learned to trust.

The change of path let me have an active social life and become a valued member of my new community, playing a role in the Student Union and the campus. I studied hard, and the University supported my goal with a luxury stipend, so the material part of my life was arranged on its own. The level of stability made me believe that my previous life was so hard because I was meant to go through the experience to be reimbursed later.

The world I entered was mine. People there valued books, lofty discussions, deep study, and a passion for knowledge. Psychology began the first summer when I asked for something to read at the faculty, although specialization was planned to start in year three. My future mentor was kind enough to provide me with the most boring giant-sized book, and I soaked it up like a sponge, convincing him of enough love for the subject. Completing year two gave me another possibility of having a private timetable evaluated between the biology and psychology departments. My classes were mixed with higher-level students, including from specialized courses that would otherwise not be part of the teaching. It was an unforgettable time with so much new information, discoveries, discussions, and work done, as well as so many interesting characters and life situations. The love of entrepreneurship had not been forgotten, which I now included in my research. My half-course paper has been published twice in regional journals, with the opportunity to present findings at an international conference.

In the 90s, the topic of psychological factors determining choice in favor of entrepreneurship soared. That was the core of my research, where I explored underlying motives that push us to enter entrepreneurial activities. I argued that these are not basic and monetary needs but an inner urge to serve others and the realization of self, supporting the hypothesis by the summary of interviews. It was impossible to measure my condition when I presented my findings at the conference, advocating self-realization. I clearly understood that a conference panel of professors doubted my idea. The jury chairman took the stage to summarize their point of view, saying it is difficult to be guided by self-realization when the turbulent economic situation pushes people to find meaning in spending on food. He used his own entrepreneurial project as a sample and concluded that even professors should provide for their families. The hall froze, and it seemed like my whole life had flashed before my eyes. With the professor's every word, my undervalued self was falling when suddenly I heard my voice. I blurted out this stupid question: 'Would you start your project knowing that you would not get paid, just with the bold belief that others badly need what you are offering?' The pause went on for eternity before he said just a few words that changed the situation. He said that he would do it anyway.

Most sensitives are naturally shy and have self-trust issues, as we doubt our opinions. It is so because we can see a situation from every possible angle, making us naturally believe that every argument has equal value to become possible truths. However, it makes it intrinsically hard to form our point of view, and we must spend enough time processing and preparing. We must play out all possible scenarios before we can convince ourselves that this is what we believe. It is also true that we change our opinions like crazy, following thousands of others' voices before we learn how to listen to our own. Do you remember that feeling when the discussion door is already closed, but an 'aha moment' suddenly happens, and you understand what should have been said? Such situations often occur with sensitives. Unless we know about it, we treat ourselves as damned. Understanding this ability, however, allows us to take it easy when we need time to decide and be free to ask precious questions.

We are often afraid to offer our point of view, being shuttered by others who have more confidence, and it takes time before we understand that confidence has nothing to do with competence. Competence, in its turn, has nothing to do with the ability to see a situation from a different perspective which is as important as certain narrowed, competent knowledge. It's a must for a highly sensitive person to remember that no one's discovery comes from knowing, but all are from the patience of unknowing and braveness to ask the most stupid questions. Anything we believe serves the situation, but life is a flow of change, so there is a logic in 'the more we know, the more we unknow.' I believe that only cooperation serves us best where different opinions are valued. Thus, I learned through fear that I must trust myself without prejudice. I learned that the most stupid question is an unasked question. I also proved that sensitive abilities serve well if we follow these heart-based impulses. The sky became blue again, and the sun rose, following my skyrocketed self-esteem.

# Chapter 3

# Polarities

*Life is made from polarities unless*
*you start to see patterns*

## When we are watching a movie, one thing happens for sure: the movie ends

My father was the man I breathed for with the hope that I would be the one to give him everything he deserved for sacrificing his life for us. I worked so hard for a moment to say, 'Dad, thank you so much for everything you've done for me, and now I can support us.' Overcoming his conditions, he struggled with life, not being able to let go of his life drama but holding onto his responsibility for us, who became his 'must,' his prime motivation. I know that he loved my sister and me equally, but I also know that he and I had a special bond that went right between hearts without any words. We had a complicated relationship with each other at different times. However, I remember most of all the moments when we discussed things as if we were sister and brother. He shared his tears with me and asked for advice as if I were the elder of us both, realizing that I see nuances. He was also a sensitive soul and wrote poetry in his late days. His loving hands did every single wooden detail of our home. He bought books and created our little home library, where I was introduced to photos of Jacques-Yves Cousteau (a true lover of nature) or heard the orchestra of Ennio Morricone. He was a stoic in his life beliefs, yet he was a real romantic man with a gentle name, Vadim. He was from a different time, full of suggestions and ideas which were not considered 'normal' by our society of primitive norms and habits. He faced the necessity to wear a brutal mask of artificial masculinity needed for the 'real male.'

When we were younger, he tried his best to find us a mom. This woman, Nina, so dear to my heart, came into our lives with such love and care. She had two daughters who became our sisters. The few years Nina spent around my teenage years made me a woman. She was 'the one' – a practical, artistic, skillful fashion designer with perfect style. She was the true feminine, nothing less than a queen who could cook, sew, protect me in school, and make a budget to prepare for long winters. Her presence changed everything. A vast array of vinyl records with pieces from Beethoven, Mozart, and Richard Wagner relocated with her to our house. I heard my first piccolo in Valkyries from this collection, which later helped me in meditations during my pineal gland experiments. Nina told me about a story between Wagner and Friedrich Nietzsche, pointing me to a few books of the latter, which I immediately read. I was allowed to listen to records after school and take any books from her library, a new library full of love stories and grandiose names like Alexandre Dumas, Theodore Dreiser, and Honoré de Balzac!

I looked at her with admiring eyes while she handed me nylon tights, flannel pajamas, and rainbow underwear with a new color for every day. You can imagine how my father never even suggested to us those things which belong to the woman's world. It was just unimportant to him and therefore didn't exist in his world. Nina even made me love winter, which I was afraid of with my whole being. Lying in my bed with my eyes closed, I would predict (to myself) the fact that snow would be covering the land on days when it was. This ability shows how intimate of a relationship we had with winter. I felt the very first steps of the coming cold, which was severe for one who was never adequately dressed or had enough preparation. It could be that I had cold intolerance or had some challenging episodes with cold temperatures in early life. The day snow arrived was the day of my winter depression beginning, a depression that would accompany my days until the first smell of coming spring in the air. Witnessing this, Nina virtuously changed it just with a simple idea. I remember that mid-summer day when she gave me new winter boots. They looked terrific, but I asked in surprise, why now? She shared with me the wisdom that good hostesses would buy winter stuff in the summer when prices are so cheap that half of the savings is just enough. I couldn't wait for a moment when winter came to try my new boots, which were so warm and comfortable. Sadly, the older girls of the household did not get along with each other, so Nina could not stay, which caused the home to become an empty nest again. I called her 'Mom,' and this separation was severely traumatic for me. I don't know how I survived the loss of two mothers in one lifetime.

Several years later, a faculty member knocked on my campus unit door and asked me to immediately call a dean. When I did, I heard her quiet voice saying, 'Your father died.' My world of 24 years was smashed.

When Nina left us, I was grieving for months, I thought I knew what pain was, but I was wrong. When my father passed away, I could hardly remember days. That was the pain. Pain that split my heart into halves that would never have a chance to be connected again. Pain that called into question every moment of my existence, any logic as to why I should remain in this life, any chance of being happy again. Every day I opened my eyes, turned over, and closed them again. The University community helped me to keep activities and daily routines while I felt that my heart had dissolved and its pieces would not be able to get together again. It came so suddenly, in the middle of the moment when 'all-was-so-good,' that life lost the sense of reality. I remember how I went to the room where the coffin was and took a seat by the side. I was in a lethargy where I could not produce a single drop of tears. I was sitting there for three days, killed by the voltage of pain, and could not release. It was an intense shock for one who had lost everybody. My soul plunged into the abyss.

Guilt came a few months later when episodes started to appear in my head. I remember the time I last saw my father, when I came home from the city for a weekend. That day I told him everything was so good, and we had a long night's discussion about all the aspects of my life. He didn't like a few bits, but was happy for me, and it was a good talk. I wanted to offer him a bit of money but decided to postpone it until the next time, ensuring I was stable enough. When I remembered that, the deepest guilt entered my heart for not being able to provide for him in return. That started a whole chain of memories where I judged myself for not being able to say, make, or arrange things differently. My mind was arguing the fact of the loss; the heart was bleeding. Those who remain know about that deepest sense of survivor's guilt and anger at being unable to change anything. My nervous system was exhausted physically, and I faced apathy with an absence of energy. The wall I built skillfully, mastering all possible aspects, had been destroyed. Loss swept over my life again, showing that it never left me. It was always somewhere behind the wall, waiting for the moment to be able to say: 'remember what you hold within.' For a moment, I believed I was a lucky student, privileged by the opportunity to build a new life, but the truth came back, accompanied by panic attacks making every night a survival battle.

In two weeks, my hair became completely white. I faced my biggest fear: I was left alone in a strange world.

## Unity dreams and incompleteness

It is hard to believe that everything that happens in our lives is for the best, especially in the process of grieving. In my old world, my 'thank you,' my father's expression of pride in me, my hope for a happy ending, this could no longer happen. However, the grieving process had gone through its stages, month after month, and the pain was getting quieter. Being a good man, my father treated us at the level of things essential to survival without a hint of emotional warmth. His broken heart caused such behavior based on a sense of duty. However, I wanted his acceptance, emotional warmth, and recognition so badly that I decided that I could change him one day if I tried hard enough. I didn't realize that I couldn't change another person. Instead, I imagined I could do it and receive the much-desired flow of love. The tragedy of death becomes a complete failure of this carefully crafted scenario. I no longer had a chance to change my father's attitude or behavior, so I lost the dream of being loved and accepted the way I wanted to be.

Highly sensitive people are connected with others and the world around them instantly. Thinking about the painful loss of my father makes me believe that some people are here to reconnect and feel oneness, yet some of us have come out of that oneness with a need to learn separation. Highly sensitive people often do not separate themselves, going through traumatic relationships until they understand personal borders correctly. My best explanation is that we could be united at the soul level, but in this world where we operate through personalities, we must remain 'healthy' individually.

If we are not individuals, we experience an incompleteness that often evokes dreams and hopes of a different kind. For example, it could be dreams of reunion based on the need to be accepted or remembered. It could be a lifelong quest for the perfect soul mate. It could be an idea of finding a guru to tell us what to do or a master to take care of us. It could be a wish to belong to a particular community. Once we fall short of these expectations, we may experience feelings of the other pole. It could be anger for life circumstances, the need to escape from 'this gangster planet,' the wish to return to 'our star somewhere far away' full of wise and infinitely compassionate souls, and so on. Maybe one day it will happen, but I know that reality will remain ugly until we believe that the world surrounding us is so. Until we accept it, it will not accept us.

## If you want to be happy, you need to become happy right here and right now

It was quite an autumn day, one in which golden foliage and the warmth of the wind mingled. The class was small, and the subject was quite specialized. Our professor of clinical psychology researched the topic of deviations. He was profound, dedicated to the subject, and spent most of his time with deviated patients. It was a student rumor that he would become one of them as he had been working on clinical cases for too long. His presence brought a sense of calm, sadness, and perseverance. It may be that he had a broken heart or had suffered tragedy; his body reflected no physical strength. He seemed to be holding something heavy but dear to him. Modest and tidy, he somehow reminded me of my father. When he talked to us, he used to turn around looking at the blackboard for an idea and would come back with further explanations. The blackboard was always empty. The students loved him and got used to his style because his thoughts were intriguing, provocative, and meaningful.

On this particular day, following one of his turns to the blackboard, he said something that changed my life. The professor said we need to learn how to live without leaning on anybody.

Loud beats of my own heart pulsated in my head. I got excited about this idea, which suits me and my situation precisely as if it were explicitly said for me. Two decisions came out of this:

1. be grateful for what I have right now, and stop waiting for something to happen to become happy;
2. learn how to live without leaning on anybody, so don't wait for anybody to appear to become happy.

I could not agree with that more. In other words, I decided to become happy right there and then. This episode, where I landed in a moment of the present, being pulled out of the past and the future, is one of the best in my life. I was grounded in the 'now' moment where all coexist simultaneously, as explained by eternalism. I was especially interested in this subject when I considered philosophy as a path; it was a milestone in reaching it.

This status meant that I stopped running away from my current life, into the future 'one day,' and into the past, where I still had unaccomplished experiences. If I wanted happiness, I would be entirely responsible for it. However, we tend to think of solutions as polarities, opposite qualities. For example, if the marriage is unhappy, we feel we need to get a divorce; if they didn't appreciate us as a team, we'd leave, or if we couldn't get something, we'd give it up. It was simple to decide that I didn't need anybody else to be happy if my father could not be with me. Thus, my decision led me to experience the next episode, a life of independence. Independence makes any form of deeper connections difficult and impossible, yet it took me another decade to fully understand how it works.

Doesn't it make sense to become happy if you want to be happy right here and now without anybody or anything? However, my inner emotional state did not change. Moreover, I was exhausted by losses, so I had no energy to dive deep. I built this decision on the abyss of trauma, where independence was an attachment to loneliness. I disconnected from my grief, loss of belonging, and dream of community or meaning to others, eliminating them as unwanted.

The choice to experience the second pole – the independency – made me stronger. However, I didn't exit the 'dependency-independency' polarity yet, I was at the same frequency of it still.

## Willpower and the choice

The year before this episode, I was told by the dean that the faculty might get the opportunity to exchange single students with America. She said, 'We think you have a good chance of getting this grant, but there will be a language test, so you'll need to make the most of your summer.' Indeed, the next day I spoke to the director of the local language school, asking her to allow me to study in exchange for my working hours since I did not have the money to pay for additional classes. The school was a private entrepreneurial initiative that flourished, offering professional improvements through language skills development. The director agreed to accept me for an administrative job, to which I happily agreed. I like any school atmosphere with adventure and opportunity in the air.

The grant did not make it to our university, but I made friends with the small school community, where I asked for a full-time job after graduation, rejecting my psychology path. They were kind to take me in, and days were filled with buzzy student life. We didn't have many native English speakers at school, and we tried to keep in touch with them by organizing weekend clubs and activities combining students, teachers, and native speakers. One of our native speaker guests, who we invited to the school from a business sector, decided to teach classes on the weekends because he got bored that no one in the city spoke English. He was such a hero. Almost two meters tall, with a broad American smile that never left his face, he became the center of attention for everyone at school. His classes often spent time together at school, even after classes, and got together with his wife too. We became friends and even went out together from time to time. One day, he asked, 'Could you help me find a marketing and sales deputy?' I had good connections and started asking everyone around, telling people how fantastic this opportunity would be to work with Rick.

One day, my friend looked me straight in the eyes and asked: 'Are you crazy? It's a unique opportunity, and he knows you well, so why don't you try it yourself?' An electric arrow pierced my heart at her words because it could be a dream job – tutoring, opportunity, and luck all rolled into one. I didn't understand anything about marketing and sales, so for the next three days, I interviewed all my friends on sales funnels, marketing programs, analysis, and customer needs, carefully writing down everything I learned in a small notebook. I couldn't sleep, I couldn't eat, I couldn't drink, I just wanted this miracle to happen. I asked for a meeting on the fourth day and made an offer. We had been talking for so long, with questions and answers going back and forth, me showing everything I had learned. After midnight in their living room, the last words cut through the air: 'I take it you don't know anything about this. But I see how much you deserve it. I know that you are hardworking. You have a chance, but the final decision will be with the CEO, come to the interview tomorrow.'

Closing the door with an enthusiastic, benevolent secretary smile, I again felt that feeling of life's movie. I don't know how it all turned out, but they accepted me. This time I not only met one of my angels, but he also became my business teacher. We played it by trial and error with a team. We went for brainstorming coffees, hooked up to local TV channels, made forecasts and argued with the finance people, built relationships with big corporate customers, hired bartenders who achieved the best sales, and did plenty of other crazy stuff. It was a time full of sparkling startup turbulence, which could hardly be forgotten.

It was one of my most significant chances, of which tail I'd get a good grip on – good luck in my real world. The only need was to learn as much as possible, which I was not afraid of, being ready to work 24 hours a day. My superhero avatar was starting to build muscles! It was the beginning of my adult life when I fully realized the idea of not relying on anyone. Closing my sleepy eyes at the end of the first working week, I heard the same voice asking, 'what about psychology?' 'I need to take care of myself now that I'm alone, so I'll be back at the age of 40.' My voice, school, University grant, and the smile of my business angel, all drowned in a bottomless ocean of deep relaxation. I slept for the next 16 hours.

## Life of dreams becomes a very true reality

My investigation of the business world was full of magic moments. I was chosen as the best Nokia country sales representative for the sale of the phone model, which that same year was popularized in the film *The Matrix*. I received an invitation from their headquarters for dinner. Management invited me to participate in an accelerated finance training initiative provided to top regional marketers when I traveled to Colombia. There was an article published in the local newspaper about a rising star being selected for the President's Young Managers Initiative, which, yes, was sent to my maternal grandmother. The British Council grant allowed me the United Kingdom SME internship, and the Warwick campus won over my heart, where I got an MBA from the business school.

Only one point was lost to the Spanish 'Clickair' when I represented the first national low-cost airline project in the European competition. It was an opportunity for me to present a startup project to the European Bank for Reconstruction and Development and make a fortune fundraising with one of the oligarchs. Becoming Co-Chairman of the Customer Relationship Management Association, I traveled the world for about five years, speaking with international conference organizers. So many opportunities were realized; for example, to create an MBA client relationship course and teach it.

I met so many big minds; for example, I had lunch with an entrepreneur who, a year later, founded the best alternative bank in the country in partnership with Goldman Sachs. Some of them were well-known, and some were behind the scenes. One day I answered a call from the Treasury Secretary's office asking me to pass on an invitation and discuss with Sir Richard Branson's team the possibility of him participating in the National Economy Summit. The air around me was always full of bubbling ideas and unlimited opportunities. For example, what a gift to launch the first national co-branded card for Visa with such a fantastic multidisciplinary team. Teamwork was always at the center; we spent time with the crew in Salt Lake City and popped in for the day in Las Vegas.

Some of the projects I was involved in were unusual; for example, I got to experience arranging a visit for the sheik as a member of his team in connection with the launch of company operations in two new countries. Some were just memorable; for example, when I sent a smile to the President, who shook hands with all the gentlemen around and said softly: 'We don't shake hands with ladies by tradition.' Beautiful and adventurous years, just like the stories from my books. Friends made fun of me, remembering Maverick.

Fifteen years later, I parked my red sports car outside a business center in the historic center of a capital city. There was no one around; I was alone, by the privilege of the general director, to plan the time of work. Sports cars are very low, and if you have ever tried them, you know that before getting out, you need to make a specific movement and adjust yourself to be able to get out of the car. I opened the door, about to leave, when wild pain shot through my spine. I couldn't move; my back was almost paralyzed. The dramatic morning conversation still echoed in my ears with a laudatory male voice, 'who do you think you are, a star?'

A few weeks later, I found a crazy doctor who had rehab centers for former athletes to help them recover from injuries. He dared to publicly refuse spinal surgery and help many to heal through physical muscle development (yes, through pain), saunas, and ice water. Every day after two to three hours at the gym, I had a walk in the park for my back. This day was especially vulnerable, and I could not hold back my tears.

For a year now, I had been in a hurricane of destruction in all aspects of my life: financial, personal, career, and psychological. Lost and broken with no faith and meaning in the life I was building, I never felt the loneliness closer. I remember the moment when I entered this business life. How happy I was that I had been given a chance, how bold was my teacher, and how encouraged was I. How and when did it happen that I lost myself in all these meetings, presentations, dinners, tennis cups, galas, and endless decisions? After the word 'decision,' I distinctly heard the phrase, 'I will return to psychology at the age of 40' in my head.

I was 41.

# Chapter 4

# Games of Personalities

*Understanding mind games could shrink a few*
*decades of your search for the source*

## I came here by disconnection from my true self, which I judged as 'not good enough'

Where did I hear that question, 'who do you think you are?' It sounded so familiar, I thought, and I had a flash of memory the next moment. She was a lady in her 50s in the bank's chief accountant position. My task was to find out why the conflict arose in the team of that bank and who caused it. That was an agreement with the bank's President in exchange for the opportunity to conduct my research. It was a small private bank; I think the whole team was only about 20 people. By the time I met her, I had already interviewed almost everyone, combining work on conflict with personality tests and all the metrics that I needed to do. It was easy for me to understand what was going on as I was allowed to talk to everyone, and although people didn't say anything directly, I could read between the lines and ask the right questions. Other people called this woman 'gray cardinal,' meaning her influence acted covertly.

She was powerful, straightforward, and out of limits in telling people what to do, which was not always in line with the bank's President's policy. The internal conflict was the usual corporate power game in which she defended her dominant position. One day the door of my office was opened, and I was met with a large body, followed by feelings of anxiety and a lingering depression. To start, I asked how her morning was. The lady gave me a complete account of how she tried to navigate between her neglectful husband, who refused to help with a trip to school, children who needed care, and colleagues whose calls started way before regular working hours. It seemed to me that she could not say no to anyone trying to satisfy the world around her in exchange for importance. I said, 'It's so because you're being too kind.'

The next moment, my trembling hands poured water into a glass to offer to her. My client started to cry suddenly with such force, as if it were the last day of her unfulfilled life. Her large shoulders heaved like mountains of the weight they carried, and tears flowed like a river down her face, which had forgotten how to think about itself. Later I was introduced to the concept of 'anchor,' which is used in psychotherapy. Anchoring is a process by which any event – sound, word, hand raised, intonation, touch, image, expression (known as triggers) – can be associated with some reaction or state and trigger its manifestation. A positive anchor is an anchor that causes a resourceful state and pleasant experience. The negative anchor is an anchor that causes a non-resource condition and unpleasant experience. As a natural empath, I catch the trigger word and inadvertently verbalize it without thinking about it. This word destroyed the whole structure of her personality, built on the idea of artificial kindness.

Conventional psychotherapy cannot cope with such intensity. For me, it was a shock. All we could do was talk, discuss, analyze, repeat, and so on. I did not know how to stop it or direct the current situation into healing. A part of my mind was alarmed because that woman opened up in front of me. We were taught to behave with patients so that they did not rely on a psychologist by sharing their inner states, because this is the most dangerous situation for the patient who can develop a strong dependency. The other part of my brain repeated, 'you haven't been trained for this.' I ended the meeting somehow, having been triggered myself.

She seemed so distracted; how could I tell her that her 'kindness,' known as 'do-goodery,' is not good at all? Feeling stupid, unprofessional, and without any life experience, what could I say to her? 'Who are you to even say anything to her?' this voice in my head asked. I had nothing to answer. 'You spent five years getting the education of your dreams with the idea of helping the world, but you couldn't stop just one woman from crying,' these thoughts destroyed me. I didn't have children, my relationships were a disaster, I didn't manage a team of professionals, and I had nothing to discuss about the life tragedy I had faced.

On my home that day, I decided I could not be a psychologist. My dissertation was approved to build on my previous work in entrepreneurship, and I graduated with pride, but deep down, I felt I wasn't good enough for my chosen path. Honestly, I gave up, feeling like I didn't have the right to tell people the reality of what was happening. I could feel, understand, and explain it, but I was intimidated by this episode and didn't feel I could speak openly about it. 'Who do you think you are to tell others what is happening and what to do? You are nobody' – with this decision, I closed the door of my fascinating university years, finally obtaining the title of the best student of the faculty.

My return to psychology was a promise to the Universe. It was a decision, and it was a proven contract that I never fulfilled. A glimpse of understanding started to appear.

## Your ego's most sophisticated trick

On one particular day, my friend, a broken but still brave soul, invited me for coffee. He was one of those people you recognize from the first moment, with a feeling of close connection. He told me about Bhutan, its nature, and great insights, and showed me the crystal-clear gems that he arranged to become meaningful spiritual jewels just this month. After a long pause, he said: 'Come with us. These guys helped me to find the light within.'

It was a lecture at a Kabbalah center. 'Kabbalah' comes from the Hebrew word meaning 'tradition' or 'received knowledge,' and Kabbalistic thought is often considered Jewish mysticism. The next day I met with a member of the community. Answering her questions, I repeated yes, right; I left psychology because I could not answer the question of who you consider yourself to be. I had no experience, and I was not a professional. She didn't let me finish, and said: 'this is the most selfish question, the superpower of your ego.' Wait a moment. I tried not to overstep my limits, to be humble and kind, not to jump over the people around me, to work for the result, and never speak for myself, so now she tells me I am selfish.

It was like a slap in the face. Remembering the soft power of the question, I asked what it meant. The lady explained it to me so simply and so meaningfully. It was like somebody explicitly organized the whole situation, from the call of my friend to the conversation in the cozy coffee room of the Kabbalah center, where there were a lot of books and people reading around me – all of this was for me. It was a concise explanation of the concept of 'nobody.' Imagine that you are a vessel of the divine, and a spark of this life passes through you. In the middle of the flow, you suddenly stop it by asking, 'Who are you to do/say/ participate/experience this?' This planet is still a planet of free will, where you and I can stop the spark flow by choice. However, who are you to ask this question, being a vessel for the divine, judging it, and deciding what is right for you and what is not? It isn't straightforward to recognize such a judgment associated with modesty. However, we are meant to understand that if we do not appreciate what is given, thinking and dreaming about something else, we are simply betraying ourselves. I remembered the morning before the back pain attack and that question that hung in the air. It signaled me to move straight ahead! I left with deep gratitude. Although I did not become a follower of the Kabbalah or any other teachings, I respect the spiritual search within any discipline.

## I am not my body, and I am not my mind

Disconnections work. It is a mechanism that helps us overcome the obstacles associated with situations where we lack energy. Every time we don't have power, it hurts us. Disconnecting from emotionally charged situations helps us conserve energy to navigate the world. It is a defense mechanism that helps us overcome the obstacles associated with emotional overflow in such a way that it does not solve the problem but creates a distance between us and the problem so that we have a moment to rejuvenate. Remember Scarlett O'Hara's famous line, 'I'll think about that tomorrow.' This decision has saved many highly sensitive people who are easily overwhelmed. Disconnection gives us time to get more resources, although this is not a solution.

If we want to find a solution, we need to go back to the point where we made a solution; the same door serves as an entrance and exit. The decision we make in difficult circumstances becomes the step we need to keep going; it saves us. All decisions are relevant to experienced circumstances. Once the situation is changed, those decisions no longer serve us. We often refer to them as 'limiting beliefs.'

Beliefs are ultimately related to the emotional complex created by a difficult situation. While many people report that the elimination of limiting beliefs technique worked for them, it depends. We may endlessly repeat, 'I am not my body, I am not my mind,' but real change can start only when we realize the unity within body, mind, and soul. My observations show that any solutions based on the mind work solely as a band-aid until we are triggered again. It's just a matter of time before emotions return. We are triune beings, so processing must be done on all three levels: blocks in the physical body, mental decisions/beliefs, and emotional patterns. It is helpful to work on any of them, but it is invaluable to release all three.

My way of connecting with the point of need for release starts through the body, just like in Vipassana – you may have heard of this practice, which could be described as a form of long dedicated meditation, connecting your attention to bodily sensations. Our body is an open subconscious, always ready to help; here, the wisdom of the Buddha is indisputable. After emotional release, doing fantastic work with the mind gradually becomes possible. The beauty of our essence glorifies, and the possibilities are endless. The ability to trace a limiting belief is considered almost an art.

For some people, feedback occurs over a brief period of time; for some, it might take a few years. In my case, it took more than a decade. We absolutely should not be afraid to return. First, life never sends us into situations we cannot overcome. Experience does not matter; only the emotional pattern does, and this is the second important point. The problem will never be the same, it will simply be the same emotional cocktail we need to process. Remember childhood fears that we outgrow? Just like them, through strength and energy, problems we move past will only make us smile in retrospect.

To work on a decision, we need to accept it and stop working against it by labeling it incorrect and eliminating it. Many will hate their 'limiting beliefs' and seek to get rid of them. Many will say this is not mine; someone embedded this in my childhood. My belief is simple: I take full responsibility for my life, including the time spent in my mother's belly when I couldn't decide what to absorb. However, we can only intake what resonates with us; otherwise, there would be no cause. Instead of creating demons, we can try to free them, which means our shadows can become our best friends. If some limiting beliefs appeared in my life, I resonated with them. I consider resonances good, showing which exact place I was artificially protected before applying healing or emotional processing.

Instead of eliminating them, we need to accept our old decisions and beliefs, validate them as correct for past situations, and thank them with a deep understanding that the decisions work as a defense that we have created. If we are strong enough and no longer need the protection, the decision could be released. However, we must dive back into the problematic situation to ensure we are healed and base our solutions on healthy emotions. We don't have to put in much effort; life will still bring the same emotional cocktail when we are presented with tests, so why bother? The third point is that if we don't want the actual situation to happen, we can force emotional work mentally. In this case, we could make sure that we process emotions and transform decisions by doing psychological work intentionally.

In my situation, the scale of the disconnection was large. I didn't accept my whole true self, doubting it, being useless to help another, and making the decision, 'I'm not good enough.'

Our unique combination of emotional, mental, and physical indicators makes us the path. Therefore, we can only go so far, and nothing is outside us.

## The person who makes things happen

My mind identified happiness as a success and translated it into money, status, meaningful work, recognition from colleagues, 'prizes and medals,' the launch of a family, and the birth of beautiful children. I gradually stepped up the ladder of a long list of social expectations. At the end of the exercise, I had a family, a high-profile job, a complete package of a perceived happy life, and a feeling of loneliness and depression like never before.

We view loneliness as the opposite state of belonging or connection. We build social relationships based on typical values, such as having a partner, working in an office, or being a member of community groups. However, I was not alone. Science pointed to a new trend in which people with many friends and who live with families still feel lonely, and the case is significant. Experts at the University of Minnesota have predicted that loneliness kills more people than obesity and alcohol, which has been said to be vastly underestimated. The future of loneliness, scientists and scholars predict, is a type of layoff unless one learns to reconnect with oneself, each other, and the outside world on a new level. I understand that this sense is not social loneliness but detachment from self and loss of belonging, so healing starts with reconnection with the self.

My artificial happiness didn't leave me much time to think about myself or how I felt, switching my attention to the outside world. My career had jumped at an unpresidential pace, and I had never lived a better material life. However, I started to notice something. I would meet many people who would say 'I'm good,' with difficulty explaining what 'good' meant. In other words, many around us find themselves in an emotional state where they don't feel emotions. I call this state 'energetic lethargy' because emotions reflect energy flow. There was no flow in this 'I feel good'; it was like a stagnant lake. Any recharge sources, such as fitness, special dietary supplements or vitamins, nature trips, stress relief by gatherings, or entertainment, support the steady-state vital energy level. Stop all this, and one will feel very hard without an external dosage of energy. Such a stressful life becomes the norm for us, where we believe a moderate stress level means that we feel good and are in control.

The global change called into question the need for a constant level of stress. I am writing these words after the great pandemic, when most of us found ourselves at home, with restrictions on the usual way of life. For some of us, this became a nightmare. However, many realized that they would like to change their lifestyle to a more casual one, even at the expense of a stable monthly income, simply because it is less stressful. This situation rejuvenates the concept of well-being, pointing to a balance between the various sources of a happy life and not just monetary values, which created 'normal' stress levels. The economic concept of wealth based on insatiable consumer needs has been challenged. The search for new forms of post-growth life has begun under the pressure of climate change, social inequality, resource depletion, biodiversity loss, and the honest question, 'what ends do we desire?'. People suddenly realized they wanted sufficiency instead of efficiency, new forms of supportive communities instead of exclusive club memberships, and life in nature instead of artificial society ladders.

We ask ourselves who we want to become. In my case, I became a person who 'makes things happen' – the best appraisal I have ever received in the business world. I knew what, when, how, and with whom to enter this world of 'doers.' To explain, I enjoyed my life as a 'doer'; nothing was wrong with that. The thing is, my personality understood that the game was over. I won the challenge for which I created my avatar. Do you remember that each personality is made for a purpose? Once such a purpose is achieved, we need to transform. That was the moment. I wasn't inspired, I didn't appreciate what I built, I was in deep stress and depression, and I lost my meaning because everything I made was done without connection to my true self. I missed this company, I lost this connection, and this was a cause for my loneliness. I saw a vision of my super personality as a big, strong superhero with hands holding the tiny lifeless body of my true self, barely breathing.

'To act, to create a challenge, to change scenes, to cling to new people, to start a new storyline' became empty for me. Nothing was attractive in the corporate jungle and entrepreneurial landscape anymore; I didn't feel it was real. It was not my world; I no longer belonged in this place. I succeeded, was proud of myself, and was ready to understand the next turn. It was a masculine world where being sensitive equaled weakness. I realized changes in myself that I was not proud of, and I could not make many decisions in favor of something other than profit.

'Show me the money, baby,' they all repeated the same story. The intelligent voice asking if I was an intuitive leader was a rare exception. I was tired of budgeting, implementing, building, and making earnings for shareholders' satisfaction. As a pioneer in relationship management and a proponent of responsive service, I was heartbroken when the owners and managers told me I did not need to bother if our sales were all right. It was true for the time being, and many ideas did not fit the situation yet. At that time, nobody knew of community-led growth, so the corporate world and the realm of private business lost my interest. I went out and closed the door on everything I had earned there.

Seeing how everything related to the 'artificial self' collapses is excruciating. I lost it all, but I stuck with my belief in a flow that requires 'giving' in order to 'receive.' Many people have experienced such moments, and many books and stories have spoken about dramatic life changes. For many, such episodes become a breakthrough point; people are reunited with their true selves and start a new, happier life. For many, this becomes a point of no return.

'It is so stupid' was the comment of my friends, colleagues, and former partner. It didn't matter to me as I got my freedom.

## We all have a particular amount of energy given at birth to find our gift and become a (re)source of ourselves

My true self was lost and forgotten, but my decision to return to psychology was alive. I packed, and we moved to Cyprus to live a simple natural life with kids. Life, where every morning,

I could ask my neighbor how his swim went yesterday, eat fresh seasonal vegetables, walk along the coast, enjoy the smell of homemade oven-baked bread, and maintain an excellent level of education. I had a huge task to return and become who I am, and these horizons made me wake up at night and make my heart beat.

When my mom was pregnant with me, my parents took a long cruise on the Black Sea. I think the salt water was calling me back to the sun and the simplicity of life. I significantly reduced my material possessions but started a new path of self-knowledge. Indeed, it was again a new life. My sixth life.

I am a lifelong learner, so I upgraded my coaching and counseling skills through a two-year professional retraining and became a trauma therapy practitioner. Day after day, life became interesting again; I found great joy in emotional processing. I excelled in processing and increased my processing speed so well that lifelong episodes could be released in an average of 40 minutes. I am endlessly grateful for all those who stood with me during this process, letting me achieve about ten thousand practicing hours.

My life episode with the gray cardinal made me smile and have a tender feeling of acceptance of myself, the lady, and the whole situation, which turned out for the good. I hope she finds or has found her ground for life. I found mine, able not only to transform any intense feelings but already to master mental constructions. It was no longer just an emotional processing but understanding of cause-and-effect relationships, which was breathtaking. The healing process becomes the process, where emotional processing was the first part and work with the transformation of limiting beliefs the second. Every session was like a story from a book, but even more intriguing because it was from the real life of a real person. It's hard to believe in the design of games created by our minds. They are fascinating and also form groups, like in a neural network.

I was ready to be back as a psychologist when I was on a flight to London, sitting by the aisle. My neighbor was a man in his 80s with wild gray hair, just like Einstein. He argued with his wife that he needed a drink. A crew member was around, so I ordered two drinks for both of us, offering them to him as soon as they arrived. He was pleasantly surprised, so we spent another four hours chatting. Between us, there was a warm feeling of long-standing connection and a subtle understanding even before someone said a word. He was a Professor of Psychology from an Australian University; imagine how lucky I was to get his opinion on the topic. At the end of the flight, I asked him to advise a person who would like to return to the profession. After a short pause, he warmly said, 'Try ... not to judge people.' Such fantastic advice! I am still grateful. I consider that little episode the synchronicity that happens when I turn to my true path. This sign was meaningful with a glimpse of the magic too. Imagine how wonderful it was to get all my answers nowhere else but up in the sky.

The impact of emotional processing is profound. My mind cleared up, my body became noticeably younger and healthier, and my sensitivity increased. I captured a lot more gustatory, olfactory, tactile, and even auditory nuances. My preferences had changed, and my taste had become different. For example, I could no longer use or smell mass-market perfume, sticking with a few chosen brands that mix natural aromas. My perception of time changed in such a way that I would feel when it was the right time to do something, or when it was better not to even start because it would take longer, have additional steps, or would not work out at all. I felt what was mine and what was not much better. For example, many people talk about the time between three and five o'clock at night being good for meditation; it was working as a destructor for me. In my case, I feel a connection at sunset time and before sunrise. There were days of straight lines and those when it took longer to get into the state.

I kept experimenting with emotional release and its consequences daily, sitting for two or four hours. Not only could I feel the decision in emotionally charged situations, but I also experimented with the acceptance of beliefs. It is fascinating when we accept a legacy of what is no longer needed and lay down a new idea that needs to be in place. Once limits are off, the following base comes by itself; we must sit and feel what is coming patiently. It is much more interesting to take things as they come than it is to give directions on what (we think) we need.

An interesting transformation happens following the process of observation and understanding. When we understand another person, we can easily accept the position of any player in the situation we find ourselves in. Therefore, there is no judgment since we understand all of the roles. I think I've reached the point my professor of magic pointed out.

Everything happens on time, but the first two years of work on the reunion were filled with tears and pain that would be enough for a few thousand people. Emotions were very intense. That's all I could feel at first, but I decided to accept it with love. Gradually, I became aware of different feelings in different situations; my emotional keyboard became more accessible. My unfrozen emotions, which had overwhelmed me before, began to melt like a piece of ice on a river when the spring sun stretched its warm, caressing rays to the river water.

On its own, an increase in sensitivity has a profound effect on the curiosity we have about experiencing it. Being in touch with yourself and doing what you love is also essential. I define love as an engagement on all levels: emotional, mental, and physical. Imagine that you spend your whole life doing something that does not light your heart. How boring would it be?

Once I connected to myself, I could feel an essential contrast to my personality during life situations or experiences. Being more in personality, I always experienced discouragement once my planned tasks were fulfilled. I needed something else to fill the void. Do you remember I told you about a sense of emptiness after success, salutes, and greetings, followed by empty days and feelings of sorrow? My observation is that when we connect to our core, the joy in everything we do begins to manifest without time limits. It happens in such a way that even when we accomplish a task, we do not feel like we have completed our achievements; therefore, we do not feel an emptiness afterward. I had a feeling of stepping on a new mastery level. I am the master of my life; you are a master of yours. By mastering our life, we can connect to an infinite energy source, enjoying what we do endlessly; therefore, it is essential. Since I have gone through this experience, it has become quite evident how we relate to energy. We could receive energy from the outside world, but we are constantly in need without this internal connection. However, once connected, we feel the flow of energy from within. We stop consuming, no longer merely surviving, and are no longer in need of external energy. We start a life of joy in service.

This world could be called the world of pain and pleasure, which is very true, but we can manage our lives in such a way as to rise higher. My case shows that this could be done through emotional processing, when we release our experiences so that only the wisdom remains with us, allowing us to understand what is happening around us. I know many striving for liberation who have given this word its meaning; I offer mine. It has made my days freer and sunnier, with such a simple understanding and without any unique discipline, medicine, or rituals, so why not try it while following what you want. I once assumed that any episode when I couldn't process my emotions was trauma. Working with trauma as a known phenomenon with practices from psychology, I enriched its meaning with knowledge from philosophy, spirituality, and my findings. I am openly sharing all of this with you now because I believe that each of us is destined for more and can begin the journey of mastery in our lives at any time.

I have had many teachers in my life, and many words of wisdom have encouraged me. There has also been enough pressure on me to change the path I have taken in life. If we know how to listen to life, we are always safe and know what to do next, being just a simple vessel for the great flow of love that follows through life. I can't even imagine what else is possible, but I'm sure it's deep, so I continue. Why don't you join in or smile with me as you pass by a step ahead?

# Chapter 5

# The Gift

*We need to get ready to accept our gifts;*
*otherwise, the price is too high*

## I will remember that apple forever

It was a collective guided meditation where the trainer used a specific story to drive individual experience. Guided meditation is a form of imagination work where we are fully connected with our feelings and emotions. It is called 'managed' because this work involves a ready-made script. This one was aimed at finding gifts that we all have. The group spent several days preparing, so everyone was fascinated by what was coming next, looking forward to a deep connection with themselves and meaningful insights. For a long time, I tried to understand the meaning of my gifts. I considered myself useless as a child since I had no spark inside. Whenever I have done psychological or spiritual work on my gifts, it usually ends in nothing. I'm sure it didn't matter much, but I couldn't figure it out. Any work, be it hypnosis, most profound meditations, or conscious affirmations about my giftedness, was in vain. I opened thousands of imaginary gift boxes, entered hundreds of doors, and imagined dozens of versions of my best self, but nothing worked.

Starting meditation on this day, I was so excited because it was a long time since I had asked a question pertaining to gifts and I had done a tremendous amount of preparatory work. I was ready to hear something significant and prepared especially for me!

Lying in deep relaxation, bathed in sensations and music, I walked along an imaginary path, stepping along a mountain lake. The voice said that there was another house, and someone was waiting for my visit. Step by step, I found myself in front of a wooden house and, entering it, saw an ancient sage. He sat on the bench and got up as soon as I entered. He was like Merlin with a long beard, gray linen dress, skinny and tall. I looked into his warm blue eyes and said I am such a tired father; I have come a long way looking for the gift of my life. They said you have something for me. Yes, he said, give me your hand. A fresh, fragrant, green, and large apple touched my hand. He gave it to me and so deliberately closed my arms. Take it, dear; what else can I give to someone who already knows everything. He turned, and so did I because the bell was calling us back. The meditation ended, and I returned to the room where everyone shared feelings and visions full of sparks and gifts of abilities, possibilities, and opportunities. My hand was holding an apple.

We tend to believe our gift will be revealed someday if we persist. We work so hard in the absolute blindness of what is within us, what already exists and always has been. We have often been told that we're not good enough yet and must work to become someone with a gift. No one said that our job is to look inside ourselves and appreciate what is already there. Before my mind started chattering again about uselessness and mundanity, I took another look at my hand. The plain green apple was so brightly fresh that I could physically taste the sweetness of its juice on my tongue. He had said, 'who already knows everything.' Did I just forget about it? I was ashamed.

The very next second, my whole life, the feeling of pain, the ability to feel thoughts, and the physical taste of an apple all clicked into place: sensitivity! My gift is sensitivity. I've tried every door except one that was wide open for me. I knew I was sensitive, but I had no idea it was my gift! I was born with it, and it has been with me all my life. It individualizes me; it was my worst enemy one day and became my best friend the next. I had thought the best thing was to keep running away from it. It was an enlightening moment.

## Do you remember the time when nobody wanted to be sensitive? It made us vulnerable, ashamed, and alienated

Grown in a warm atmosphere, high sensitivity benefits the individual and society, adding a unique value to its biodiversity. However, the ability to feel every minute nuance of the surrounding world is a heavy burden for those who do not understand. Highly sensitive people don't choose what to take; they feel everything. There are ways to deal with this because too much information causes emotional overload. Unable to handle this large amount of incoming information and take care of themselves, highly sensitive people struggle with it. This is significantly related to vulnerable children when they acquire so much that they cannot handle it becoming 'uncontrollable.' Unmanageable and uncomfortable for adults, they receive instructions rather than simply understanding. Imagine that instead of a positive validation, the child will receive a negative one, confirming that their behavior is not approved in the family, school, or society.

For this reason, many from a very early age begin to hide their gift or even be ashamed of it. My case was the same, except that I was not a hyperactive child; I was deep inside. My sister told me we could both get a room cleaning task, which always took me so long that she yelled at me. I wasn't present because my mind was somewhere in the clouds.

Creativity goes hand in hand with high sensitivity, but in my case, I didn't excel in any of the art classes, which was to be expected. Therefore, I decided I did not have a spark, although it was simply blocked. If your child seems sensitive, please never give up on their quest for artistic ability. My other social problem was my inability to express my thoughts directly or react quickly. I needed time to process everything before I was able to give my opinion, and while everyone else had already said something, I would be sat still. These situations branded me as shy, and no one bothered to ask me the question again, so I kept most of my answers to myself.

High sensitivity is still not well-known, and some may even wonder what kind of disease it is. There is no illness at all; this is a character trait. If a person with this ability does not know about it, they will not be able to use it or appreciate it. However, my experience shows that if a person is told they are very sensitive, they will confirm that deep within they always knew about this. For me, this is a sign of internal validation, but we are always looking for it from the outside. With male sensitivity, the situation is even worse. It has been socially forbidden and shameful for such a long time. Because of this, we have raised generations of emotionally blocked men asking for understanding and love from frozen hearts. Blocked sensitivity can be the source of difficult personalities who perceive the world as dangerous and have a stronger desire to change it. Overwhelmed with emotions and not knowing what to do with them, most simply block them out. Emotional blocks are associated with various types of psychological trauma. Some trauma may have been responsible for names with negative connotations in human history that we will never forget. We can shame them, but society and social rules are in control. The more we understand this, the more sensitivity will be accepted, the more empathy will be allowed, and the more hand-holding will be available.

The good news is that things are already changing. Sensitivity was considered a weakness in the era of Individualism and traditional industrialized 'world of things.' However, we are witnessing the birth of a new 'world of senses' where connections to nature and social equality are back-ordered from our past when people lived in harmony with nature. These days we value empathy and inclusiveness for the Future of Work, collectiveness, where sensitivity enables emotional intelligence, creativity, and innovation. We could not survive in a world where economic growth has depleted planetary resources and world power structures are still fighting for the rest using old-fashioned games and solutions. However, every end is a beginning, so we are witnessing the birth of a new order. The era of the earth as the single home for everybody, resurgent nature, knowledge, and eco-technologies has already arrived. Scientists from various disciplines, be it economics, anthropology, ecology, physics, or engineering, are all looking for the best solutions for post-growth paths. Entrepreneurs and earlier pioneers' social propositions are rising, prioritizing the Experience economy where experience prevails over material purchases and, therefore, the economy decouples from natural resources scarcity. There is nothing more demanding these days than to become more and more sensitive.

Today we strive for creativity and innovation; it has become a trend. However, whether highly sensitive or not, a person can be creative, as long as they are safe. When we feel unsafe or insecure, we switch into survival mode. Survival mode is an adaptive human body reaction that helps us survive danger and stress, while stressful stimuli cause a specific physiological and psychological reaction. This mode involves releasing stress hormones and activating our stress response systems, so we can't be truly creative in survival. A sense of security means that we do not expect harm or pain, physical or emotional. Individual psychological safety is the understanding that we are in a safe space and is a crucial term for creativity and innovation.

Following much research and literature on psychological safety and its creation, especially in the workspace, I would like to draw your attention to the word 'perception.' Perception is an individual characteristic, meaning how you perceive your world or psychological safety in our conversation. Perception is individually controlled, being personal.

To simplify, someone can be safe and unsafe in the same environment; it depends on individual perception. Self-perception regarding paying attention to feelings, clarity of feelings, and restoration of mood is nothing but emotional intelligence – moods and feelings based on initial emotions that, you guessed it, can be corrected or reworked. Indeed, it is still vital to maintain psychologically safe places, but not to forget about personal responsibility for emotional instability and vulnerability.

Connecting with our emotions and being able to recognize them is the first step to being able to transform emotional states. Attention to feelings refers to how people view their emotions, and clarity of feelings refers to how people think they understand and process them. When we disconnect from selected emotions, we block access to the entire emotional keyboard. But if we deeply connect to the chosen emotion, we will unlock the whole keyboard; this is a twofold technique. Therefore, any work on emotions will make us more sensitive.

Researchers define highly sensitive people as those more strongly affected by what they experience. Therefore, we must unlock sensitivity virtuously to remain sensitive without becoming too vulnerable. These days people are not afraid to be vulnerable and are starting to use that to show their true selves to others. To some extent, one can even say it has become fashionable to demonstrate vulnerability, especially since the pandemic crisis. However, the degree of vulnerability matters and people also appreciate vulnerable stories with happy endings, meaning that the hero overcame vulnerability and found a way to become emotionally stable.

Therefore, emotional intelligence has recently attracted public attention. Emotional intelligence promises to teach people to recognize emotions and deal with them. Some scientific papers confirm the connection between high clarity of feelings and a high ability to restore mood. It has also been stated that the ability to process emotions can be learned. Working with a professional should be a first choice, but once you succeed (work through the most difficult emotional blocks), your daily practice could become personal. We need others sometimes, but many sages consider emotional processing to be an individual practice. It is a process that connects us with sacred moments of unity with the self. If the other person needs to be with you at that sacred moment, this is your choice.

The other trend is that emotional numbness, which causes loneliness and disconnection, cannot be considered a healthy part of life. Once welfare was considered the norm of society, numbness helped overcome the problems of morality and social responsibility, helping to make informed choices in favor of personal gain at the expense of others. An emotionally disconnected person could feel satisfaction; this is correct. However, welfare has been seriously questioned in favor of well-being. The concept of welfare focuses on the economic outcome that helps people get more money to satisfy more insatiable needs.

In contrast, well-being includes a broader family of variables such as health, home–work balance, or rich social relationships. This distinction is not consistently recognized, but it is important, indicating the need for a balanced wheel of a happy life, where economic significance is only a part. In addition, it was stated that we want economic equality and well-being for all.

Most of the suggestions for well-being are related to social responsibility and the ability to live with others in a community. The ability to feel another person, which allows us one day to predict the behavior of another and form larger societies, overcoming tribalism, becomes a priority. It can be said that the chemistry of the human essence has changed because we gradually moved from pure satisfaction of needs and dopamine achievements to a mixture of oxytocin, which is responsible for caring, kindness, trust, and prosocial behavior.

Do you remember my story about pain and the red sports car? I often think about what could have happened to my life if I had gotten out of that car and done it as usual. I feel so much gratitude for that episode, considering it my wake-up call, and I want to cheer up everyone who is going through a difficult moment right now. Please keep in mind that this may be your most prominent call for the better. It is especially true for moments of loss related to people, money, property, or business through betrayal. It is so because the outer world is just a reflection of our inner world, and people treat us the way we treat ourselves. If we face betrayal, it's always because we're betraying ourselves, so why keep weeping? Raise your shoulders with gratitude for your understanding and boldly walk into a situation that used to make you weak.

## The way home

The new life was insatiable for inner work. It's fun to think about it now, but it was a deliberate process. I did one emotional release session after another and wanted even more. Our emotional body is intimately connected with our biological body, so physical conditions improve once we work on emotions. However, you need to know that the body is not like the soul, where healing occurs at the speed of light. It takes time to catch up; mine was two to three weeks behind the psychological work. It couldn't take more; it needed rest and so much detox. It is where all my childhood knowledge from my father about herbs, natural remedies, and body care surfaced. The muscles at the back of my body, my entire spine, and my legs were as hard as metal. The flip side is connected to our past and was an absolute reflection of the shock and fear I faced, including my panic attacks and nightmares. Lying on my back, I could barely lift my legs. Having formed a hook, they remained bent in a hopeless attempt to get at least a 90-degree angle. Now I could swing them back freely in Halasana or 'plow pose.'

To increase the intensity, accountability, and support, I started a social project, combining work with other people, inviting trainers of new techniques, and organizing groups and courses. I felt helpers everywhere, and information flowed into my hands in every possible way. People started giving me names, and emails, suggesting places to work, becoming volunteers, or becoming clients. We have tried many tools and techniques, such as holotropic breathing, yoga, various meditation types, trauma therapy, hypnosis, family constellations, aromatherapy, cryotherapy, and physiotherapy. We tried it all, combining bodywork with psychology and spiritual practices.

I had my flow with an internal connection through a process that I could best describe as meditation. I used to sit to feel what was needed, ask, and offer help to myself. My task was to feel a place in the body that would work as a door to an episode needing clearing or emotional processing. I did not do anything extra but simply continued my emotional processing. Soon after, the place would appear with physical sensations such as pain. The next task was to feel what emotions were not processed there, but then it became a rabbit hole with a new understanding of what emotions were grouped in baskets.

My mind has never been afraid to take information from one place and put it in another; that's what happens with what I call 'emotional nested baskets.' I got acquainted with the term 'nested baskets' when I participated in a project for a low-cost airline. As a non-industrial project manager, I needed to be trained in all aspects of aviation. A representative of the ticketing system pioneered in low-cost aviation explained to me one of the principles called fare/ticketing baskets. It just means that each fare will fit in one basket, and you can't move to another until you sell all tickets with one fare from one basket. After the sale, the basket becomes unavailable. Even if someone cancels the purchase and returns the ticket, it will be sold at the price of the existing basket. Thus, the fare will be related to the demand, so when one variable (demand) increases, the other (fare) will automatically increase. There will be no cheaper fare. Emotions are stacked in similar baskets so that when you feel one, the other is unavailable. However, once processed, lower basket emotion will never happen again and be available; it is gone.

The beauty of the quality in the work of processing emotions makes it irreversible. After treatment, the injury could not return. If you looked at trauma as any situation where you don't have the energy to process emotions, that would make even more sense. Once your energy level in this situation returns, you cannot access the lower energy level of the emotions because you are on a different level. You can mentally remember the emotions, but you will not feel them with a traumatic effect, and your body will not record them. Emotional attachments would not exist anymore.

An interesting thing also happens if you are open to working with others. First, once you work through something in your own experience, the next person to show up for the session will have the same pattern as the one you just worked out. It feels like we're not separated, and when one does the work, it reflects the many. Second, you will never meet a person who demands a job you have never done. It means that we can only see what is in our fields, what we have already processed; other types simply do not resonate. When I worked intensively, I also had times when I processed something without being able to remember a direct connection with my personal experience. Emotions can be inherited, or we can feel them for someone else. If it comes, it resonates with me, and if those emotions call me, I will work without any questions on the task that is allocated to me.

My openness to experimentation was rewarded. I was introduced to another fantastic ability we all have if we become sensitive enough. It is the ability to feel situations before they appear in real life, known as precognition. I felt a few of them, such as the death of my colleague, attempts to use my time and skills for someone's gain, or massive social upheaval. I think this work could be accelerated if one is interested in the perfection of the prediction degree.

Would I trade off my new seventh life, knowing it would go through betrayal and loss? I needed to let go of the situation and devote time to other meanings than business achievements, a career, or the fact of marriage. I realized I had a massive debt to myself because I had rejected my gift of sensitivity, judging my ability to carry it on. If we are not ready to accept what is given, then the price is as high as the answer to why life should be maintained in a body completely decoupled from the meaning of the same given life.

# Chapter 6

# Experience

*We believe we are here for learning and experience,*
*but it turned out that this experience doesn't*
*matter at all*

## There is a very popular belief that states we are here for an experience

When I started my emotional work, I just wanted to release my pain, but I was granted a miracle of a much deeper understanding of sensitivity and emotional power. Let me explain how we completely misunderstood the meaning of experience. Everyone is familiar with the popular notion that we are here to learn and gain some experience. This belief is based on the idea that we need to navigate life, and therefore we go through the experience of learning. Experience helps us to make faster and better choices, become available to help others, or transform into better versions of ourselves daily. The question I asked was when it would be enough. Why am I losing all the people I love or am engaged with? I was so young when I was separated from my mother, from both grandparents due to divorce and relocation, from my older sister Oksana, whom I still love and help, my second mother Nina, my father. My personal life shows no differences. Why are we trapped in repetitive experiences? Why don't we start to experience anything else as being enchanted by the same?

Something was missing in this concept. I needed to stop the pattern, which I could not survive anymore. People who start to recognize patterns should question this experience theory of existence with persistence; otherwise, life will happen to us again and again. That means we will remain victims of circumstances without the knowledge and ability to change the cycle. The idea that came to me was so bold that it surpassed all my fantasies. It has been said that you need to treat your mind with big questions if you want it to work to its full potential, and I took a risk. Whoever follows the same path can experience Eureka moments as I did, hanging the question in the air with humility and respect for something greater than ourselves. My question was simple but very emotionally charged for me. I asked, 'what do I need to learn from the losses of all dear to my heart?'

An answer I received may be a pearl of known wisdom to some, but each of us lives in our world, so any knowledge needs to be grounded in personal reality. Mine was enlightened with the thought that we are here not to learn or get even more experience but to get rid of it; more precisely, from consequences of past experiences or unprocessed emotions related to it.

## My grand finale

I was still lost in my uncomfortable, painful reality. My task was to free myself from this vulnerability, where I desperately needed the opportunity to sound different. Yet it was very, very deep. So deep that I knew that I was afraid to find out the truth because it could be destroying me. I felt like a survivor who would rather keep the pain sequestered within than touch it again. At the same time, I knew it would change my life, so I prepared day by day. We need to understand what is possible when starting the journey. Many would advise grappling with emotions and overcoming them. For example, many fear simple things like making a video, expressing our feelings openly, or calling for an apology. By overcoming this fear, we become stronger. You can be pushed to face your fears, and it is okay. The pain, however, cannot be overcome. It can only be processed. Please don't push yourself into pain without resources, do it gently and be patient. It is beneficial to know that life will never allow us to connect with situations we are not ready for; this is a wise teacher, so there is no need to push anything artificially.

I had a scary feeling of something harsh profoundly affecting me, and so dangerous that it vanished without the slightest sign in my conscious mind. I understood that it would connect to the unconscious and that life prepared my energy level for this. Whatever it was, I needed to be prepared, because I would be faced with an episode that left me speechless. My life loss experience targeted nothing but this. I thought it was a conditioned birth trauma, the memory of which was difficult to recall. Emotional work could be done only by connection with unprocessed emotions and not by empathetic cognitive understanding. I needed that connection and asked for it, meditating for hours daily.

I use mental time travel, which scientists call the brain's ability to think about the past, present, and future with specific effects such as 'chronesthesia.' The Cambridge

University researchers from Clare College first introduced me to this concept. My personal practice let me understand the concept of mental time travel as imagined or mentally executed travels to any episode you want to access. You may also call it the process of remembering, which includes future episodes if you think of time as a cycle, not the arrow or line. Any mental trips generated, whether by AI virtual reality, imaginary, or life experiences, could be liberating, but it is a matter of emotional connection.

Anyone practicing mental time travel also needs to understand the metaphor and how it works. If we cannot recall the actual episode, the mind will supply us with visions that have a good chance of not being like the episode but producing the same emotional pattern. Mental travels require strong coherence with the heart, where emotional engagement could prove the relevance of the experience. If we see visions without our hearts emotionally engaged, it means we are dreaming or imagining. Visions could be used metaphorically; however, emotions would make them real. Images without emotional engagement have no connections with us; they are irrelevant until we establish a contact point. Our target with emotional processing should be the activation of emotional engagement.

Next, I learned that we must find emotions affecting us and release them before we touch mind constructs and the belief system. Change of the belief system, which we lay down on the old emotional pattern, requires constant attention and management discipline, so we control our essence and ensure we don't touch unconscious – this is very energy-consuming. I consider a change in the belief system to be more beneficial based on an unattached emotional state. In this case, it makes us more open and flexible without flashbacks and rigidity. Rigid belief systems put limitations on us, while flowing belief systems let us adjust to the change process and align with current situations. This change allows us to focus on adaptation instead of resistance. We adapt and do not use life energy to control the world around us or our own mindset.

The emotional processing work is similar to trauma therapy, which concentrates on bodily sensations and emotional release. However, mental work is in line with mindfulness techniques. There is a third part of the work, which I will explain later as spiritual. I have decided I need a combination of all, being open to anything with sincere intent, to find the cause of my repetitive pattern. One day it was granted with meditative vision.

I took another step along the path from the top of the mountain to the village. I had just arrived and was going to meet my people, with warm anticipation of reunion. I had a feeling I was absent for quite a time. Mountains left and right, trail down, a great body of water sparkling in the dawn under the bright sun; I think it was noon. This feeling could be experienced by those who returned from the desired journey but were happy that it was over, glad that they had finally returned because everything had been finalized. I had village shoes on my feet and bracelets on my hands, something like what the indigenous highlanders wear today. I checked our tree next to the path; we had a hiding place where we left messages for each other. Waiting for me was a quartz crystal, our symbol of trust, our sacred object we never left alone. They seemed to miss me very much, as they had left a stone here. I felt tenderness in my heart as I love these people deeply. My steps were getting faster, and I was in a hurry to hug them all. Great, this is the last turn on the path. The next moment I saw them all. Dead.

My legs were no longer holding me as I collapsed next to the one who filled my heart. My soul, my love, my friend, my brother, my teacher, my life. He was the first to lay his head down with his arm outstretched forward as if he was trying to bridge the space and reach me out of it. I realized that the crystal was left because it was returned to me. It meant that love was back. It was my freedom to live further. I think he knew something was about to happen. The whole village was there, not so big, about 20 or 30 people. They lay as if they had been switched off, with no sign of panic, attack, damage, or battle. It was as if a laser beam or some other kind of technology had turned them off simultaneously. They would not fight in any case; this people were highly polarized by the idea of any use of force being impossible even in defense. White dress colors showed they were ready for the meeting; they would talk and share their problems. I don't know how much I cried there. When consciousness came back, it was night.

I felt that deep feeling of being left alone, which is so familiar to me from this lifetime. I lost the meaning of existence; my heart was broken into parts, one of which died alone with these people so dear to me. Sudden memory brought up an earlier episode full of buried village smells and reflections of the fire. I felt the child who had her life saved just because she was sent to the forest by her father and left alone. Once nobody came to pick her up, she came back to realize the truth when she felt something horrifying was meant to happen. She could not save them, which followed deep guilt about being alive while they all left. It seems the pattern of losses was deeply embedded in my emotional body, and it was not one lifetime I struggled with.

Someone raised by love in another family would have the same feeling of losing their new family. It could be that I was adopted by those people wearing white clothes. I had a feeling that I belonged to them. However, they were different, although we had strong ties. I went through a few more details later, but it was the central episode where I felt the most pain. I told you that our minds do not distinguish between real and unreal episodes. It does not matter to the mind. I have no idea what it was, past or parallel, inherited or absorbed, but I have never felt this level of real pain while experiencing any loss in my real life, including the biggest of them – my father's death.

This feeling of loss was not new to me when I encountered it. I knew that I had lost someone. However, I could never explain it because I did not understand the source of this feeling before. I knew I didn't want to live, yet now I could feel the decision when precisely I was detached from myself by 'I don't want to live anymore.' The next moment was oblivion, and it was my own choice.

The connection to that episode helped me release the capsule of my emotional trauma, and my life has changed forever since then; that was the end of the pattern I had experienced for years.

## Our perception is very individual

The book stories played such a significant role in my life. I think my mind mainly absorbed every possible course of action and every possible way out of difficult situations from books. At first, they became the basis of my inner world, which became my shelter. They also made me believe that one day someone would come to rescue me. At a later stage, they honestly showed me that the world around me is much more complex and ambiguous, so they became a big part of my painful awakening. I awoke from the biggest illusion in my life of what the world was doing wrong, realizing that this was only my world that was not in order, and I was responsible for that. My emotions, such as shame, guilt, anger, grief, and pain, ruled my life.

However, books show me enough stories of people whose lives become good after disillusionment. Analyzing my connection with this cloud of information obtained from books, I have become more and more convinced that we choose to see what we want to see or resonate only with specific things. If we consider life as a flow of information, we could observe it as a flow of personalities, situations, knowledge, and circumstances we encounter. For a psychology student with a love for philosophy classes, this becomes an important observation to understand that there are no objective realities in the human mind. However, each is the only reality to the individual. Everything we perceive is related to ourselves, so it would be true to say we perceive the world through the veil. We stick only with specific people, situations, and circumstances. In other words, each life is individual, and there cannot be two identical experiences even in the same case.

My broken soul perceived the world as a very dark place, hoping to meet another light one day, seeking this sacred light in another – my father and other close ones. Many believe that hope helps us in our darkest moments, but if we want to be reborn, hope is the last thing we can rely on. If we want to make a breakthrough, it must be precise knowing, firm belief, or direct choice to take full responsibility for our feelings. During that process, we need faith that everything has hidden meaning designed for us with love, and this could not be what we hope for. However, hope is the feeling of the sunrise. It makes us believe that a new day will bring us a new life that will fix everything, spending our lives waiting for 'one day.' I was not destined to fill my heart abyss with somebody else, and the life force wanted something different from me, pointing to home within.

You probably heard the story of seagull Jonathan Livingston who was destined to become his shining self without a chance to be accepted by his tribe. My favorite moment is when he decided to accept himself at the expense of loneliness without a hope that anybody would follow him. He went through intense feelings of unacceptance and frustration that he could not persuade others to join him. He took a chance that allowed him to meet his peers, yet he needed to give up on the hope that others would fulfill him first. He did so by concentrating on self-development, nourishing his feeling of freedom and happiness from his mastery. He was able to genuinely connect to himself, the same destiny that awaits anyone who will step on a path of emotional power. My vivid dream helped me to see my disconnection and understand the causality; moreover, it helped to open the door to healing.

## Reconnection to self

My research revealed that if I want life changes, my mission is to arrange three things. The first is to find the most emotionally charged situation and release it, processing emotions, to free a space for a new information/situation/episode. Once we have no emotional tensions, we can not fully access the second point of limiting beliefs, which prevent transformation from happening. In my case, it was essential to touch the point of most emotional charge accessing the situation of trauma encapsulation. It was also crucial to understand that any decision we make will be in action unless changed. Decisions are the backside of free will, which could become a limitation. Our decisions are reasons for repetitive patterns; therefore, if you already notice unwanted repetitions, you may try to understand mental reasoning. Sometimes, it is challenging because we simply forget decisions and beliefs which drown in subconsciousness. It is also hard to change beliefs mentally unless emotional engagement is in place. However, I never met a case where a person could not recall or change a decision made after emotional detachment.

When I decided that I didn't want to live anymore without the ability to carry on with such a significant loss as part of who I am, I formed a base for all future experiences. Therefore, in my world, any loss was traumatic, triggering earlier episodes via an existing emotional basket holding lots of grief and pain. Please bear in mind that we could go through identical experiences, but other people's situations could also influence us if they trigger an emotional response.

Mindfulness techniques made a lot of sense but did not work for me in their entirety. To observe an emotional state is not to release the emotional state. Relaxation or attention, awareness (which could even serve as re-traumatization), and even mental acceptance are not the core goals of meditation. Meditation is a connection to the self, and the self combines all, including our emotions. When we try to direct our thoughts despite emotions and without alignment with emotions, we try to heal in disconnection. Life will push us through situations that need to be emotionally processed anyway; nothing to worry about. Still, do we need all these fearful and stressful situations to appear in our life to be healed? The same is true of emotional releases – without change in the belief system, the effect is temporary. I firmly believe in the united approach: union of heart- and mind-based techniques.

It is a well-known belief that we access our gifts by facing our biggest fears, and I consider this to be true. My biggest fear was to be left alone, because in this case, I felt most of the pain, grief, and being so close to my limiting belief that I didn't want to live anymore. Life has thrown me to that fear again and again so I could overcome the tidal fear barrier and access that feeling of abyss of pain so I could go through it having more resources and more energy. My inner work with emotions, visions, metaphors, and mediation worked well, so I finally faced that fear and went through it. Since that session, I was not involved in any loss situations and didn't even think of it. My relationship with break-ups and even death changed dramatically. The same work could be done in any other case. You probably would be interested in knowing what I did after mine, as I have already mentioned the third part of the work.

I cancel the old decision being thankful for its role in saving me at once. My body had no tension, and my emotions were calm. I gained an understanding of the last piece of work, which is reconnection with parts of myself. These dissociated 'parts' are known in psychology as shadows; in spirituality, they are called parts of the soul. What is the true essence of these 'parts'? Are they parts of conscience, mind, heart, or body? These parts of us hold the unprocessed experience we don't want or have no energy yet to connect with. Once emotional work is done, these parts can be reunited so we do not feel broken anymore. We unite because there is no need to hold anything apart longer. Many describe unification followed by feelings of peace, safety, or security. To me, consolidation has the utmost importance, and it doesn't matter what we call these parts because if the job is done, we feel good. However, I found it authentic to name them as the parts of the soul, which are fragmented by emotionally charged episodes that must be recollected and reunited in such a way as to feel wholeness. The more we are whole, the more we are emotionally and energetically uplifted. We become non-attached yet emotionally engaged with life.

This work gives you so much joy and sparks that some become seekers searching for places where else it could be released and harmonized, not as a ritual but as a loving intention or self-care. It is like an ongoing loving wish to feed yourself with tasty food or learn something new daily.

After emotional processing, we feel moments when we don't need anything. Therefore, I am saying that the needs-development path is finite; the needs-based psychology construct has limitations working as a basis for our motivation. At that moment, we could decide what we choose instead of what we need. Wishes, unattached from our artificial needs, are beautiful, creative, loving, and encouraging for many! I wish we all reach that state where life could be based on those clean, detached, yet engaged choices.

For me, it was the point where I reconnected with the feeling of joy. I searched for it for many hours and days, but couldn't just find the tail under my own decision 'I don't want to live,' limiting myself from this process of sparkling flow we called life. I reconnected back, and I am so grateful and uplifted. It worked! Never have I felt such a profound sense of unity and belonging to the magic of the Universe. My joy came back to me following the decision that I wanted to live, healing and rejuvenating my emotional connection with life, which I stopped seeing as a source of pain since my life scenario reached its 'grand finale.' This began a new life, but not at the level of the previous personality.

I have been changed! Like my beautiful seagull Jonathan Livingston, I found myself the very exact moment I connected to it.

## Dream within the dream

The last piece I want to explain here is for practitioners of the mind time travel technique, those who strive to reconnect fragments of the soul, and those who are curious searchers for mind games. Any situation could have a double bottom, like a dream within a dream. The pattern was fully released once I was able to combine the whole picture, including the earlier metaphor of a child's life saved by being left alone. In this episode, my mind combined safety with being alone; I called this association. Associations need a release the same way as outdated mind decisions because unless you do that, it will attract situations associated with a primer – survival. I believe associations should be a notion of NLP (neuro-linguistic programming) as this technique works with belief transformation, but I am not a specialist here to tell you exactly. In any case, 'being alone equals safety' was worked out by the realization that it glued to survival one day, yet safety is safety, and being alone is being alone. I needed to manifest a new state where I could be safe without being left alone or attracting anybody who would remind me about that by leaving me alone. In my case, this cause and effect formed a perfect loop.

You already know how vital our survival is for the mind and body and how precisely we rely on what lets us survive – survival mechanisms written down to our very core by evolution. Whatever saves us in this life will be remembered and passed from generation to generation to maintain life. Biological evolution is the process of survival mechanisms curation; however, to be psychologically safe and to survive in the physical world are two different notions. In my experience, I needed to survive or find my safety psychological state, which became associated with being left alone; that was my recipe at once. However, when I was left alone, I started to feel pain, grief, and guilt of having survived alone. This state pushed me to decide, 'I don't want to live anymore,' where I could not execute this decision alternating by oblivion. In my life, any charged situation ended up with a deep, deep slip and oblivion or mechanism of psychological repression. However, I needed safety, so my search started again, leading me to a known solution of being left alone to survive, and the pattern repeats. The result was that safety wasn't possible at all, so I got used to a steady-state level of anxiety as many sensitives or empaths do.

I enjoyed working with that pattern and appreciate how our beautiful minds work. The reward of freedom from anxiety was priceless, and my search for inner safety ended.

# Chapter 7

# Messages

*From the ancient time, it was considered a*
*big mistake to harm the messenger*

## How open are you to the messages in your life?

When we feel intense emotions, the first thing we do is try to stop or hide them. A lack of understanding leads us to disconnection and suppression, with the motive to 'be civilized.' Societal rules support the idea that our tears need to stay inside our private bedroom because we all must keep the concept of a happy life outside. Explosive emotions are uncomfortable to observe and scary to feel. We can be ashamed of ourselves and our feelings or judge ourselves. We also fear everything which we don't understand. However, we must know how we feel, even if we don't understand it. I believe that the context of experiences or situations and all people in our life are just messengers. If the message is not received, it will be repeated until we finally get it. If you just assume this might be the case, would you allow yourself to be truthful about how you feel, or would you like situations to repeat themselves repeatedly?

When something happens, we give importance to it and the people involved; or to the image of an unfulfilled self, we prioritize it. Once the preference is given, thoughts about that situation will settle in our heads, and they will become like tenants using our mind space without paying rent. We let them in, and we spend our energy on them. Therefore, it is honest to say they own us, and we give our power away to them. However, neither the situation nor the people who carry messages are critical, but our emotional response has a vital role.

Our emotions serve as messages of what we have inside. All the rest helps us to reveal it. That is why they say that we do not forgive for those who are forgiven; they may not even be interested in it. We forgive to set our hearts aside from hate, shame, and judgment and free ourselves from heavy burdens. I sincerely believe there is a loving force behind any context, which is organizing life with an intense purpose. This purpose is not so simple as black and white, or good and evil. The outcome doesn't sound important at all, but what we feel is. This loving force points out the beauty of what we have inside or our unprocessed emotions. We don't always understand that and can abruptly interrupt the process or sink without a clear agenda, struggling to find a way back. Our task is to feel the connection, remember the pattern, and process it. However, it is a massive question of how open we are to deal with our emotions.

We stop the process of emotional release in favor of acting to do something to change the situation's outcome, which we cannot agree with. We disconnect from emotions, creating energetic walls between us, unable to feel them. These walls are needed to save us from discomfort. Every such mental construct needs energy that will support it. It is like any idea we try to manifest, requiring everyday curation and exceptional attention to become true.

Similarly, these walls around uncomfortable feelings need to be constantly maintained, a process requiring energetic resources. If we collect a lot of unprocessed emotions, our energy will be consumed to support these walls, resulting in a deficit. The body starts to react, the immune system doesn't work anymore, and we face diseases of 'obscure origin.' Sometimes our organism even begins to attack itself. Response of the body shows that resilience is over-signaling with symptoms. If we could read those symptoms, we could navigate emotional processing, leading to a natural healing process. Yet, we forget how to listen to inspirational messages and start to believe that steady-state depression is a norm in our life. We think we could deal with it later, trying to sort out more and more things around us without understanding that we cause those things relentlessly ourselves.

Life messages always exist, and it is a matter of inner decision to pay attention and prioritize your state over anything else to catch them. People often say, 'you need to put yourself first,' which is very accurate in light of emotions. Priority must go to personal messages of emotions to live a long, happy life. There is no need to put yourself first in anything else, but this is an ultimate responsibility for your own body, health, and perceived happiness. There are always a few excellent messages in any situation, even in such a severe one when society doesn't accept public emotions.

First, emotional publicity is usually reflected in people becoming sorry and pitiful of others; this is precisely the opposite of what is needed for a person in the emotional abyss.

It is so because we forget the true meaning of compassion, we have no access to knowledge about compassion, and we tend to judge instead of being compassionate. Pity is when we see a person as inferior and try to help them be better because we feel sorry for who they are. 'Do-goodery' is not so good at all. Sometimes, remembering who we are is painful but needed for crucial breakthroughs. We must not forget that compassion has nothing to do with pity for somebody, or feeling that somebody has no strength to deal with the situation. This way, we put ourselves in a patronizing position (and will eventually deal with the consequences of it in our own life). It took courage to be humble in front of life forces and believe everyone is appropriately equipped to deal with any situation. If you want to give a hand, offer it, but with a belief in the person, an inner wish for them to become free, and a sincere belief that they could take a gift from the situation. Such internal support must be applied first to ourselves, starting with permission for emotional release.

The second good thing in emotional publicity is that unacceptance is a good reminder that nobody else is responsible for our inner emotional state. You are probably very familiar with situations when we say, 'she makes me crazy,' 'he is impossible to stay with,' or 'they are such and such' – these conversations spiral us down. If you think of others in the emotionally charged moment, this is the most appropriate moment to put yourself first because our state is more important than how others are. Such thoughts are a great reminder that we need to slow down and get work done, starting with the question, 'what do I feel when he is impossible or she is behaving as crazy?' It is the right moment to put yourself on a pedestal and stop hiding in thoughts about others. This is a moment to face the truth of what is happening inside you. This work is sacred, inner, intimate, and social unacceptance of strong emotional releases reminds us that we cannot be intimate with everybody else around us.

The last good thing is a reminder that energy connects us all, and emotional arousals influence the common energy field, which everybody has responsibility for, each at the personal level. It is not that you are accepted only when you feel good. The raw truth is that we must stay in control for our own benefits and support the joint energy field without attempting to lean on anybody else with a total capacity.

We all need personal time in heavy moments, yet we all can deal with it. Disconnections from our emotions are not good nor are they beneficial to the people around us, and emotional processing must be embedded in any culture. It must become a common understanding that we could become vulnerable and need time for processing. Time for inner work must not only be socially accepted but remunerated in such a way that people become hunters for emotional self-care.

I firmly believe that social acceptance of emotional vulnerability should be uplifted and written in the United Nations Universal Declaration of Human Rights. It could sound like an article, 'Everyone has the right for vulnerability and is permitted standard emotional processing and equal pay for it, which is very beneficial for adequate health and well-being of a person, their family, and their surrounding community.' The best thing we could do for each other is to take care of our emotional health. In this case, your projections will not be placed on others, and you could see the world directly without clouds of the emotional veil.

## Emotions reflect the level of personal energy availability

There are almost no emotions that we experience as new in adulthood. All of them come as reminders of what we keep within. We cannot produce anything that doesn't exist or belong to our world. Part of it could be related to personal experience. However, another part could be inherited or picked up from others, especially if you are sensitive and don't yet recognize what is yours and what relates to other people.

Why are emotions so unique? Emotional engagement allows us to keep memory connected to people, situations, and experiences that matter to us. Emotions are tied to particular messages, and only situations still emotional for us are available. The fact of remembering says that we value something, we care about it, and it is important to us. We remember episodes, even if the experience is not essential, because they retain emotional patterns. These patterns serve as an entrance to what is real and meaningful in our world.

By the end of their life, many people notice that their only significant meaning is how they feel about life events. They assert that it is not about how they act, what they did or did not do; it is about how they feel. This is the only real baggage we have and will carry. All the rest will stay. Emotional baggage is so crucial that it is a known fact that emotions can be inherited. Imagine you process it all so that you have no attachments to any low-level emotions and don't even remember any failures or harmful situations. All you will remember is what energizes you, makes you smiles, and keeps your heart warm. What would it be like to take this state back with you?

Emotions always correspond to the level of energy we have. Long-term patterns reflect our mood, which shows the direction of energy. It goes out of us when we lose energy or inward when we receive and utilize it. So, it's wise to get in the habit of asking, 'how do you feel?' instead of 'how happy you are?' Happiness is a concept of the mind; emotions never lie. What matters is not how good or bad the emotion is but how emotions fit the current context, and if they do not, then we need a release from the past, more specifically from the emotional baggage of the past, which is a massive task for each life.

Every time we are involved in different situations, perhaps with a higher energy level and more information available, we are equipped differently. Being different does not mean being worse or better. Our task is to be flexible enough to meet new circumstances because we cannot prepare ourselves for all new situations; we don't know what will be required yet. We could get better at engineering, but market changes will follow the need for farmers. We could get better at posting rapid growth in sales, but the mainstream would change to anti-consumerism. We could maintain a perfect garden, but climate change will dry it up. We might even have great stocks, but the market crash will burn them out. Any personal remedies correspond only to known situations. Flexibility or adaptability is a meter of energy available to us; when we are 'in resource,' we are flexible; when we are not, we are somewhat fragile and rigid.

We better take care of how we feel. If we don't like it, we have a choice to do inner work on our emotional state. There is an alternative suggestion pointing to an external solution that could make us feel better. It could be an achievement of a desired goal, something new we buy, someone we meet, or an ongoing process of becoming an ideal self. In this case, we turn a blind eye to the inner truth and grab an external solution for inner emotional emptiness.

## Why I don't support the idea of the betterness game

'Betterness' is one of these solutions. You are undoubtedly aware of this concept of being a better version of yourself every day. The betterness concept is based on the idea of learning. It is straightforward to understand if you imagine artisans making wooden toys. The first would be simple and heavily lined, yet everyday mastery will increase through practice and repetition. In time you would see the beauty of wooden lines being made so perfectly as if the toy had been carved smoothly from butter with a heated knife. Through honing their abilities, the craftsperson strives to master their craft every day and considers making mistakes a necessary part of such a learning process. This concept was reappropriated from mastering our abilities to mastering ourselves. 'I could even be good, but that's not enough, and I need to get better day after day' – that's the message. Many people will also tell you that they don't fail, they make mistakes in favor of learning.

The basic idea that we aren't good enough and need to become better every day doesn't resonate with me. Although I am adept at formal learning with my three Master's degrees involved in my Ph.D., and I highly value life learning, I doubt if this is the final target of life. I believe life is the continual process of evolution. Learning, for me, is a process of life itself. My opinion is that during this learning, we don't make mistakes. We act based on the best we can do right here and now, with the level of energy available to us (energy level includes skills, information, critical thinking, and so on). In other words, we are good enough for any given moment in our lives. Life is constantly changing, and so are we. Today's situation is different from yesterday's. If we have a 'psychological resource' and enough energy, we create new solutions and new experiences with the help of new opportunities. Yesterday, we did the best we could with the energy levels available to us so the energy levels available to us yesterday were appropriate for the situations we were faced with; I'm sure we have done our best. I consider betterness a game of golden shadows; in other words, perfectionism. Why else does the world not get wiser by making so many mistakes? Because it is impossible to become perfect.

What do I feel in any failure? Do I feel it was a necessary mistake, a kind of push to be rewarded one day? These are thoughts, not feelings. I failed and therefore feel bad! Mental reasoning around mistakes necessary for learning doesn't give me relief. My emotional cocktail consists of different emotions at different times, but the overall feeling is a closed door. Imagine you've been invited to a wedding party and have been buying presents for a month and preparing to look chic, hoping to meet a new friend. The moment you arrive at the train station, you realize that you have missed a daily train and can't be at the party tonight. The subsequent emotions would reflect my case of failure. The correct understanding is that your expectations failed. Not *you*, but *your expectations*. We only feel like a failure if our expectations do not resonate with our perceived reality, which is the only source of our satisfaction or suffering. Perceived reality is the core; we perceive it as a failure if it doesn't match expectations.

Imagine someone starts talking to you because you looked upset while drinking coffee at the train station. You become friends, with the possibility of more. How might you feel? I think you would feel great because it was the only right moment when you missed that train – you didn't need a travel solution to meet a new friend! The universe could have something else in store for you. Nothing has changed in the past; the fact that you missed the train has remained the same. Your perception has varied based on the new information received; would you agree with that? Hidden (not revealed yet) information can be a simple message: this is not your train or your door. Now imagine that you were so organized and direct that the failure of a planned trip pushed you over the edge. Overwhelmed with emotions, you might not even notice a stranger who says: 'It seems you missed the train,' and you might leave the station. When we alter our emotional state, we may find another door of opportunity, which is very near and wide open. If it is only our expectations that fail and we never do, it seems we catch ourselves in a strange 'learning process' of better managing our expectations. Ultimately, why don't we just set them aside?

We would never get a message trying to overcome obstacles towards the expected outcome we have planned. To catch opportunities, however, we only need to turn on the inner light button and see them; they are always available. If we don't, we will always have problems, need to fix something, or plan how to overcome a barrier. Some people, however, seem to enjoy the process of fixing and even take it as a source of pride in themselves. There is no right solution; it is only a decision whether you want to become your life's creator or stay a manager of circumstances. I used to like my ability to 'get things done' and enjoyed the harmonization of chaos. However, I just grew out of it one day. I did it so often that I got tired of playing a desired match of 'expectation equals perceived reality.'

Being good enough doesn't stop my progress because I choose the path of emotional release. It gives me energy and being in that resource, I am resourceful. I am still alive and experiencing situations, but I care about my emotional freedom, which allows me to understand why I am given a situation. I don't care 'why this happens to me.' It happens 'for me.' I also ask, 'what gift this situation will bring to me.' This mindset has changed the perception of my world from a harsh place where I needed to learn the best way to survive, to a place of love that gently helps me discover myself in my true power. My main goal is to feel good before, during, and after any experience. 'Better' or 'not the best' is a function of the mind's decisions. However, I'm not so interested in judging the mind. I want to feel good and be grateful. Do you? If yes, reveal what is hidden for you under layers of unnecessary emotions that keep limiting beliefs.

I use each experience to find my inner resonance and release the tethered emotions. Neglect the message, and you will never be able to progress.

# Chapter 8

# Master of Emotions

*We need to claim our emotional power back*

## Old emotional reactions will not open new doors

Let's think big: what is the purpose of evolution? Is it a development of resilience and the ability to survive? Or is it a creative process of constant change where adaptability allows us to transform? It is both because resilience is excellent for a short-term change that could pass away, and adaptability is the end goal for a long-term new norm. Most of us would think of adaptation as an evolutionary North Star. Adaptability means the ability to accept and become renewed following changes as new possibilities. Those who adapt faster get more benefits than those who hold on to the past. Think about that in terms of emotions; it will be the ability to create fresh emotional responses without attachments to any past experiences and pre-judgment.

There is an opinion that experience baggage is needed because we need to rely on the known to be most efficient and react fast in daily circumstances. This is correct for understanding how we remember the most effective reactions. Yet, if we want to get over opportunities, there is no place for known reactions, and we must start the exploration process. Exploration is unknown; therefore, old reactions will not open new doors. Survival helps us to keep information memorable and repeat or recall it once necessary at a rapid speed. However, how much does a good learner know? It must be a lot. How much does the best learner know? Nothing. Non-linear thinking, such as 'the more I know, the more I unknow,' never helps forecast a future as a linear function deriving from past experiences. Yet it serves evolution, opening opportunities for change.

Emotional baggage is related to the known, and emotional potential is associated with the unknown. Do you remember that story about a teacher who offered a cup of tea to a potential disciple and kept pouring the tea while it was overflowing? This metaphor teaches us that adding anything new to the already full cup is impossible. What an interesting dilemma; how is it possible to find a solution? Look a level up, where the meaning of knowledge will not be explained baggage but something making us even more open to new information. Knowing makes us comfortable, yet unknowing makes us capable.

Indeed, before we understand anything, we need to collect as much information as possible. Once someone shares their path, we absorb that knowledge. Then another shares their path, and we also understand and learn new from it. Once we understand many paths, a breakthrough happens so that we can become pathfinders ourselves. However, knowing how to repeat and find the same path doesn't make us wise. There is the ability to find the best possible path in any given circumstance, whatever happens, to make us pathfinders.

Indeed, we need to know the sky to see a star first. Therefore, knowledge is power. The ability to navigate through existing knowledge towards the opportunity to touch the unknown is a pearl of wisdom.

In terms of emotions, this ability applies in such a way that we need to know the emotions and the emotions of others to navigate through a social world. However, the ability to get rid of unprocessed emotions fast enough is a treasure. It is so because non-attachment lets us see the world without the lenses of the past and allows us to follow the discovery of opportunities. Imagine you have nothing but can access what is needed at any single moment, so you don't keep anything yet can reach everything. I found this ability magical. Think about mastery and inner resourcefulness, and not the external resources you have. Imagine you don't know how to make a fire, so once you get it going from nature, you would keep supporting it every second on an ongoing basis with a fear of losing its unique power, and spending lots of your time and efforts. That means you have a resource. However, once you learn how to produce the fire, you may relax, making it any time you wish – this skill becomes inner, you become resourceful. Emotional capital is not the accumulation of unprocessed emotions but the mastery, quality, and ability to make your emotions work at any given moment without storing them.

Think like an entrepreneur to decide how good it is to get capital that you don't know how to apply. Capital is nothing; the ability to manage it and create healthy business cashflows is the path to business success. As a simple example, think of anger converted to personal achievement energy, the pain becoming a power, or vulnerability transformed into intuition. We could alter any of our emotions. Emotions are like a lump of clay for creation, so why throw the clay out if you want to make a pot? Any emotional accumulation, instead, will never lead us to a breakthrough. However, if we know how to take care of our emotional capital, we could start to create from change and stop trying to cope with it.

The cleaning and transformation work is not a limit to what is possible. Emotions bring colors to our life; emotional engagement keeps us connected to life; this is an invisible string indicating the energy level available to us. A master of emotions is capable of regulating personal energy using emotional power. Therefore, it is a big deal to gain emotional capital, yet it is mastery and art to keep it working.

## Transformation of a hero's journey

Once we decide to focus on our inner world, our state and emotions processing them, we let external results go. It is very controversial for the current concept of life achievements. Everybody is familiar with the idea of a hero's journey, which states we are here to become a hero of our life, overcoming all difficulties and obstacles. A hero cannot let go of achievements and desires, because this is the final result and the only meaning of a journey itself. A hero needs challenges, and they reveal themself by overcoming them. Hero model is a result of successful survival, our legacy from past generations. Hero moment is an essential episode in every individual's life and an aspect of masculinity revelation.

Yet the hero is a lonely figure amongst evil others whom they have defeated or still must defeat. Indeed, they are all colored as bad people – otherwise heroes would look strange – so we have the perfect polarization. Even if a hero is involved in the inner battle, their ego or shadows are shown as enemies they must overcome. The hero also has an audience of fans for whom they prove their brilliance and who will benefit from their win by adoring their qualities. A hero is one who benefits the most, taking the best from the best. Being a hero, therefore, is the most desirable path, so everyone wants to become one.

When everyone is a hero, nobody is. Should we agree on less than a hero and take what is available instead of the most desirable? You need to see the 2001 film *A Beautiful Mind* (directed by Ron Howard) for an artistic representation of a decision strategy that could be used within game theory when all players can achieve the desired outcome by not deviating from the initial plan. The film's main character, John Nash, explains to his peers that if all of them ignore a blonde girl in the bar (the most desirable one) then everyone gets his girl. The case represents the win without competition for the hero position, where everyone harvested for themselves without the suppression of others. The most desired is the perception, not the reality.

Similarly, a hero is just a method, not an end goal. This understanding came with psychological practice when I met the downturn of heroic achievements and understood the inner state of people that live a desired (by many) life. Being heroes for everyone from a social point of view, they were often lost within. It happened with me, too, when I achieved my childhood dreams, celebrated them for a few minutes, and got the empty sense back. Why should I dream of a hero state if the aftertaste is so painful? Emptiness is hurtful, would you agree?

It took time, however, until I fully got an answer to why people would desire something else if, traditionally, everyone wants to have the best, be the best, achieve the best, and live the best life of the best. When I had an inner mismatch in my beliefs, I had a sense of an unsolved problem, which kept me searching until I sorted it out. I felt it physically and could not do anything else until a breakthrough happened. An unresolved situation has the feeling of there being a known solution one step away; you just need to catch the tail. It is like a question correctly asked – the answer is anticipated but hasn't arrived yet. I was confused about the hero's journey and mundane path. Nobody dreams of being ordinary.

Thankfully, my inner hero, who felt nothing but tiredness from victories, was reborn. It became a magician with a lamp of inner truth: to be at the best place is a never-ending journey where another best place always arises as a new goal. Our plan doesn't need to be 'the best,' but it must be 'yours'. It is the case for the most straightforward reason: not following the feeling of emptiness. External needs and desires are insatiable, not fulfilling, and don't give inner peace or long-term joy. We must find our place, step into our power, and reflect on what belongs to our inner world. External achievements provide a sense of great energy, which, unfortunately, is finite and require subsequent fulfillment. A hero's path is so fascinating.

However, many dived deep into it and didn't come back absorbed by that game.

Our emotional state becomes more important than outside achievements. This understanding reveals the magical truth, which sages believed. This truth says that the whole world will support you if you are on your path. In this case, nothing could stop you, as you are ignited by inner light, not because you can overcome anything; you don't need any wins. It is so because you are in a flow: all doors are open, all moments are synchronized, all needs arrive by time, and life amazingly happens for us.

The flow of support started to show up in my life, confirming that the quality of my life journey had changed. However, this only happened when I opened up to my emotions and put them above any consequences of the experience, such as victories or failures. This method allows us to feel *first* (in order to understand) and only then to proceed. We can feel what is ours and what is not. This is crucial for sensitives, who don't distinguish themselves from other people too often.

Do you remember I told you that some people experience unity and some feel separation? Sensitives must first separate to know what belongs to them; otherwise, they serve somebody else's dreams. I can say, 'thank you, it's wonderful, just not my style, not my choice, wish, friend, or place.' The inner compass started showing me what I like and what is mine. When we understand what matters to us and what we value, we focus on it. Most important, yours is yours, and nobody will take it from you as invisible threads connect you. You are destined for each other. Attention gives direction to our energy. The energy itself, however, derives from an emotional engagement which is a mark of what we are engaged in. Once we clean our 'heart clouds,' work out attachments from traumas, evaluate dependencies, and get rid of them, we can be engaged with what we love. It becomes so simple once we understand the following rule: what is interesting, we are engaged with for a short time, and what is ours, we love forever.

The right direction was chosen by understanding that the most desired could not always lead to the best for everyone. At least it was not for me. When we wish for the most desired, we wish for the same. Even unity is not the place where we are all the same. Finally, I got it. Being different is being unique in combining qualities, although we all have them. Biodiversity is beautiful because it is a tapestry of combinations available to all. Unity is not about being the same or belonging to the same tribe. Unity is a harmony between different preferences, an abundance of parts dancing with each other.

The sense that 'I am in my world, I am home' becomes more critical when knowing that 'I am the best.' The idea of heroic polarization, which kept my enemies alive, stopped. I accepted them the moment that my ideal artificial self fell short. My true self arose, opening the door to miracles. We don't need to defeat someone, including ourselves, to feel that miracle inside. Everyone is blessed in their true majesty, and we don't need to be against each other battling for the same. It saved me so much time and unnecessary attempts to achieve what I desired at the level of the hero's personality, following artificial needs supported by readily offered societal values. It became my duty to feel good, to feel at home. If you feel good, you are resourceful and can only benefit others this way. I stop attempts to build my excellence at the expense of my life energy, which are arguing rights for my hero's place. I stopped arguing at all.

## How to take back your emotional power

How can we save our life energy once we stop the hero's battles and overcome the emotional baggage barrier? What opens up when we are at our most powerful? These questions ignited my search. One of my favorite scenes from the 2000 movie *Cast Away* (produced and directed by Robert Zemeckis) is when the main character, played by the fabulous Tom Hanks, keeps breaking the tidal waves barrier. He did it again and again, understanding that this was the only way to escape the island, which saved him yet became his prison. It is the same with layered emotions, which play out as a foundation for our reactions, which safeguard us yet become our limitation. Emotional processing is not as dramatic as the scene from the film; however, we need to master it to break through the same way the hero of the film did. Once we work out collected layers, we regain emotional power and become masters of our emotions. This true power opens up exciting opportunities that sages and seekers from all over the times have been pursuing for ages.

Emotional processing is only possible when we recognize and understand our emotions. In most cases, unprocessed emotional baggage is hidden because we have no energy to acknowledge, feel, understand, or deal with it. How could we navigate in this case? The answer is straightforward: a life would point to what we need through daily situations or people. However, there are nuances.

At first look, we could consider the world a reflection of our state. There is a widespread belief that we attract qualities or people who resonate with the same. It is the so-called 'law of attraction.' In short, the law of attraction says, 'as above, so below,' which could be explained as follows: we attract that which is alike to ourselves. There is a belief that positive or negative thoughts bring positive or negative experiences into a person's life; therefore, the whole movement of positivity exists. It is not so evident in real life.

For example, it doesn't explain why shy, polite, and serving people could attract manipulators with opposite qualities. Psychologists call the qualities we don't want, or have no resources to recognize, 'shadows.' In case we are highly polarized, we attract not the same but opposite, or balancing, emotional quality. This is so because if we don't let ourselves experience some emotions by suppressing, dislocating, or cutting out from them, they still exist but deep within. In this case, we will see the truth about our covert emotional state through others.

I have often heard, 'how could it be that I am manipulating others covertly if I am serving others my whole life?' To be at service could originate from a different place. The situation doesn't mean we serve ourselves automatically when we serve others. Without self-service, when we sacrifice our life for the benefit of somebody experiencing negative emotions and tiredness, it would be correct to say we manipulate ourselves. What if we could serve in happiness and joy? All mental constructs need a check versus actual emotional state;

our emotions never lie. It doesn't matter what we do and how well we or others perceive what we do. Yet how we feel while we are doing this is the key. Others help us understand so we can do emotional work uncovering ourselves, mirroring each other – a sacred gift is given for work in pairs.

Let's consider the example of a person who feels like a victim of circumstances created by their mistakes. They would usually judge themself and live with some level of guilt inside. Alternatively, they would think they are not good enough yet, and need to learn from their mistakes to avoid making more – this is a lighter version of the same emotion of not being perfect. A person could attract guilty people like themselves, resonating with the same. However, there is the same probability that a person could attract someone with the opposite quality. Practice shows that many people believe that guilt requires some punishment. This is how we are educated by society: you make a mistake; you pay for it. Therefore, in the beliefs of many, any guilt associated with necessary punishment, is how the roles of 'victims' are attracted to 'tyrants.' The role of 'tyrants' will be played by people who provide punishment and it will be the perfect match, being the same frequency as 'victim-tyrant,' but from a different pole. Thus, this person's resonance will attract the same frequency. However, the more polarized we are, the more opposite quality we will attract because within one frequency opposite poles harmonize or neutralize themselves. Nature leans towards harmony, therefore combining opposite poles. How long we will be happy serving as a victim pole of such a system is a personal question. We will attract another polarity until we get out of polarization.

We may try to take a second pole, or jump from one role to another for our whole life, too. The more we are polarized, the more robust life situations will be. It would be helpful to work the case out in real life, yet it could be a great help to work out our inner guilt, which is the real attractor for this frequency. Our internal state is the attractor, and the law of attraction must be entirely accepted, including polarized poles. If we don't want the opposite quality of the same, we need to process our emotions and live the frequency of this emotional polarity, and our task is always to work towards feeling good.

To feel good is not just our wish; it must become our responsibility. We always need to remember that emotional state is the key to any situation, but most important is the key to the energy level available for us. Once we have a good mood, we can sort out anything; once the mood is wrong, we do not have enough energy to cope with life. A negative mood with energy loss pushes us to search to find it elsewhere to fill the inner gap. It could be 'green' sources, such as food, time with nature, or physical exercises. The most intriguing way for emotional recharge is escapism, when a person escapes from their inner reality by switching to external sources of good mood and happiness. Like pills, this only works for a while; it doesn't buy us health, it just deals with the symptoms. It is way more beneficial to undergo emotional processing. In this case, we don't create external attachments; become inspired by life, and fall in love with the reality around us without escaping.

Some people found a way to get energy directly from others, being known as 'toxic people.' We can all be in a negative mood from time to time, but using the term 'toxic people' usually refers to those who experience negativity for a prolonged period. Such people have been known for their ability to leave you empty, creating emotionally charged situations out of nothing. Being in a negative mood means we face energetical emptiness. This happens through circumstances that we cannot overcome yet. It is a situation that requires as much recharging as possible, including emotional processing work, but what I'm trying to say is that this is a state and not our nature. Therefore, toxicity could be temporary. Many would advise you to avoid toxic people, but I believe we may walk this situation tall. I refer to our ability to handle emotional ropes by being masters of our emotions. As such, no toxic people can influence us if we use our emotional stability as protection.

We would feel fantastic if we could develop from emotional protection to emotional engagement. Research has found a direct correlation between emotional engagement and subsequent mood and energy levels with 75% accuracy within a range of two or three days. Emotional engagement means we are connected to life; we value something that is essential to us. If not, it causes a disconnection, and disconnection means apathy as the highest potential outcome from negative moods. Feeling good is followed by a reward, so we don't need to be recharged by external sources. Feeling good, we don't regret if anything goes as not expected, and our resistance borders become much broader, so we accept more variations and navigate through life more effortlessly. We still consume food and exercise, yet we don't depend on it as the source of a good mood. Emotional engagement, this inner emotional source of energy, always belongs to us, always has been with us, and will never leave us. How do you feel knowing a lasting energy battery exists within you? It made my life safe and brought a lot of certainty into it, which are basic feelings needed for a good life. Therefore, it is a simple technique to create an emotional engagement once we feel below the healthy line, known as 'do what you like more or be with your beloved ones often.'

Let me add a few essential details. When we are pointing out anything unwelcomed, let's say someone uncomfortable for us, we always need to remember that this is our world, and we face these people. This is not your neighbor who faced that person, your uncle who met them, or even your best friend who is in this situation. It is all for you. Therefore, it is important to think about the reason it was given to you. I undergo emotional processing when I want people to behave differently. As a tiny hint, I always remember that others could behave towards me, mirroring how I act towards myself. Personal emotional growth is the best opportunity to leave polarities or situations unwanted.

Why should you deserve emotional transformation if it is simple just to avoid unwanted polarities or situations? Because avoidance saves us in the physical world, but we don't address the inner job. Unprocessed emotional states will consistently show up. I almost guarantee you that avoidance will lead to even more unwanted situations because now you will be unconsciously checking on it, as you were able to use avoidance as a successful tool once, and will therefore depend on it again and again. Escape creates dependency. You 'need' unwanted situations to be able to escape from them.

Therefore, they said any judgment of others would come back to you. Would you still think it is an excellent solution to run away? Many people would suggest the strategy of confrontation instead of facing your fear and beating anyone trying to put you down or even suppress you. Well, it didn't bring me inner peace simply because I was not born such an animal, and using somebody's habits didn't bring me joy. This understanding pushed me to find my way, as it would probably do for you.

We cannot change a situation that has already happened, yet we have the power to transform our inner emotional state so that we will not face the same situation again. I truly believe the life target is not to teach but to help us open up our full potential. If we want to win over somebody or build our esteem at their expense, we completely misunderstand the situation.

We should never forget that the outer world is a theater where people act a particular way just for us to see something inside. I don't want to beat, win, or conquer any of my fears anymore, I just want to accept and transform them. How will we know when we have succeeded? It is simple; we become neutral to those unwanted people or situations. They will probably show up a few more times as a checkup, but neutrality shows no emotional attachment anymore. The highest flight is to feel potential tension before the actual situation and to be able to click it down in a second, just like bursting a balloon with a needle.

I would not, therefore, invite you to escape difficult situations or confront them. However, I would never ask you to stay positive under challenging cases, although many people would find that helpful. I would invite you to feel what you feel facing a difficult situation without escapism from your feelings by mental positivity choice. Our willpower works best to protect our hearts, not to protect us from our hearts. I invite you to trust your feelings, and if you feel bad, please process your emotions until they are clear, neutral, or even positively charged and uplifted. This invitation is entirely different from propositions to concentrate on positivity as a mental choice. Although mind-based techniques might work for some people, science says the mind works at 5% of its capacity. In my case, mental intentions and willpower were useless, disconnected from the truth of the heart's feelings and body's sensations. However, I could break through using care and compassion for myself and find a way to relieve myself without denying the truth about my inner states.

We must be aware that we act according to our energy level and that any decisions are based on that. Mind decisions from the traumatic situation will be radically different from what the mind will decide during a state of psychological safety. Therefore, it is useless to follow mind decisions unless we work on our energy level. That doesn't mean, however, that I am against the positive psychology movement per se; I am a great supporter of this idea because our energy flows where our attention goes. However, I underline the holistic aspect of positivity choice, which needs to be done based on understanding our essence as the unity of mind, body, and emotions. Any work should be carried out accordingly.

## Emotional mastery

You may recognize a master by understanding where a person's energy goes. The master is the one who serves others.

I am not talking here about those who serve others, depleting their resources; this is not a genuine service. A master serves as an example of an open channel maintaining energy flow. We are all destined to achieve mastery in this regard, each in their own specific area. Once we master our abilities, a day comes when we think of paying it back, and any person achieving mastery has an ultimate inner desire and resources to be shared. It is an intention to share what you have learned while igniting your heart and making your life meaningful. A mother who teaches her daughter how to cook, a trainer uncovering our abilities to solve problems, and a leader sharing their thoughts, all represent mastery.

A mastery does not refer to cases where we have learned how to cope with things and insist others do the same; this service is from fear. A master doesn't fear anything and doesn't prevent anything. A master shares their passion and dance of the soul with others simply because it is so beautiful for themself. We always differ between the ignited heart and the next preacher in this regard. People feel the mastery of energy and want to learn close to those who achieved it, not to copy or follow them. A master energy is inviting, intriguing, pushing you to discover your own self, helping you to experience the next step in this mastership, proving the master was a bridge to what seemed impossible. It is comforting to be around masters, to take steps together with them.

What is emotional mastery? If you listen to people who step on an emotional mastery path, you will learn about energy, sensitivity, healed vulnerability, physical health, emotional empathy, strong intuition, and precognition. It will also be about the ability to reach the hearts of others through emotions, creativity, the ability to feel gaps and innovation, the ability to sense and recognize patterns, and a strong desire to serve the world as a magnificent place.

It was a widespread belief that reaching such higher states is only possible when one fulfills basic human needs first. The best human potential seemed to be a proxy for stable material life and social status. In other words, we thought we needed to create a material base first to achieve the self-realization stage after. This belief was based on Abraham Harold Maslow's hierarchy of five basic need categories starting from physiological needs, leading to needs for safety and security, social needs for belonging and esteem, and finally the search for the ideal self.

Maslow was one of our most remarkable humanist seekers who dedicated a lifetime to researching positive behavior. His driving question, 'what motivates humans?' pointed to human needs, which drive motives, and was believed to be a foundation for human behavior. The scientific legacy of Maslow has become the foundation for positive psychology. He described the hierarchical order of needs, where it was impossible to jump over levels. The path he proposed for humanity was the development of needs.

However, many chefs-d'oeuvre achieved in poverty, and sages grow by rejecting material comfort proving independence of self-mastery from material security. Entrepreneurs were ready to work in their garages without food and sleep, building ideas with an enormous amount of energy and challenging dependence on physical abilities from external energy sources. It was a passion that drove them, the highest emotional engagement possible. This creative energy goes through all barriers just the same way as spiritual people prove the absence of limitations in the material world. Sports athletes achieved the same highest engagement state known as a 'flow' during the active task. All these people feel fulfilled and live more happier moments than most of us. They have been connected to their core straightaway, without a necessity to graduate from lower needs in the hierarchical order, following their passion in life.

The proposed hierarchy also doesn't explain how human needs could be shifted to higher states in the middle of insecurity and multiple crises. Difficult times seem to ignite us with limitations and challenges when many reach the state of best human potential. We uncover our best abilities in communities, serving others. Being kind and supportive, being empathetic, we can overcome anything by learning, creating, and innovating together under the pressure of a common challenge. I believe the individual path is more prolonged, while service to others instantly helps us uncover our best abilities. It is easier to show up protecting others; in this case, we don't question what we are capable of, we do what is needed, and it seems we could do a lot. We face economic crises and overcome pandemics, and our basic needs are far from elimination; we are all in this together, which reminds us of what it is to be a human by power of choice. Prosocial behavior, empathy, teamwork, mental health, and community well-being have become the hottest topics of our everyday life. Challenges point out that needs-development could evolve into choice-development.

However, Maslow's work touched on something fundamental that was deeply recognized as a direct connection between creative abilities and psychological safety nowadays. If we are in survival mode, it's impossible to learn, think of corporate targets, feel aesthetic pleasures, or achieve scientific conclusions. The corporate world is buzzing about psychological safety, which needs to be organized to boost personnel's creativity and innovations. For these reasons, they use empathy, non-judgment, openness, teamwork, support, and mutual trust. Together we cope best, and reciprocity plays over the competition.

We still need safety and security, but the source of it has become different. Sages and entrepreneurs achieved psychological safety using shortcuts without being marked best at the lower levels of the need hierarchy. Sages did it intentionally; passionate entrepreneurs enjoyed the pleasure of the side effect of being highly emotionally engaged. Both demonstrate that psychological safety is not a direct reflection of outside reality but a perceived quality. The world is individually perceived; some people find it fantastic, yet some can barely cope. Perception is a key to transformation and is hugely dependent on our inner psychological state, which is a product of our emotions.

We all have the power of imagination and can imagine whatever we want. However, the mind would consider the situation real if we were involved. It doesn't matter if the situation is imagined or happens in the real world; we are 'all in' only if we are emotionally engaged. To alter perception, we need to become emotionally engaged, so our body reacts, we experience emotions, and we catch thoughts. Our imagination is a virtual reality that we can access without any technology. Emotional engagement makes us players so we can experience any situation and alter our perception.

The ability to alter perception becomes a base for exposure therapy work which targets the successful activation of fear structures or 'emotional engagement' to them in a physically safe environment. The higher sensitivity is, the faster and stronger emotional engagement is possible. Once done, emotions could be processed, and trauma closed. Exposure therapy is based on the ability to get emotionally engaged, process it, and release it. The case doesn't change, our past is still the same, but we free ourselves of emotional burdens, so we don't spend our energy there anymore. Therapy work is successful because we activate emotional engagement from one side and can process emotions from another. The result of processed emotions is (perceived) psychological safety. In the same way, sages calmed their mind, body, and souls, doing cleaning work first to become emotionally stable before making deep inner connections. Psychological safety is the key to our inner world, which we can never access, being full of anger, envy, fear, or any other stress response. Survival mode has no access to miracles of creation.

The core of emotional mastery is the ability to experience emotional engagement and direct it towards higher states through psychological safety. To an emotional master, it doesn't matter if emotional engagement results from positive or negative emotions; we don't need to concentrate on positivity. A master could transform states and perceived reality. Don't you see the magic of it? Whatever happens, we could be still.

By being still, we create our realities, changing perceptions. The peak of sensory augmentation is named as the access to unconventional reality, which alters perception. The ability to alter perception is a long technological search where we are seeking access to it with artificial intelligence through virtual, augmented, or mixed reality. Sensory augmentation is one of the development directions for artificial intelligence. Should we not try a natural way into it by enhancing our sensory abilities through another emotional type of intelligence?

Emotional intelligence refers to the ability to effectively experience emotions within and outside workplaces, which is defined as being aware of the emotions of self and others and having access to emotional control. Empirical studies have shown a considerable influence of emotional intelligence on work outcomes, such as leadership effectiveness, teamwork, relationship development, academic performance, and prosocial behaviors. The ability for emotional processing is initially recognized through psychological therapy, boosting its implication for having behavioral control over our emotions and being strategic in reacting to the emotions of others.

Humanity has already started this self-development path. For example, most of us understand team psychological safety and its value through the corporate world. Business is a form of collective activity that plays its role in human behavior enhancement. A slight shift is needed towards individual psychological safety recognition and our abilities to manage it without dependency on corporate arrangements. With the development of emotional intelligence, emotional processing will be in trend for the next generations. We could concentrate on self-development instead of needs-development valuing something more fundamental than money or material status, such as love, conviviality, creativity, and community bonds.

However, we still need to do the work. It is difficult to concentrate on something else if you are in the middle of a crisis – this is a bold truth. The ability to see opportunities is very timely, but how many of us can achieve that emotional freedom? Many would remember meditation experiments when a few thousand people meditate together in such a way that police registered lower levels of crime and violence. Scientists agreed on the possible connection of societal violence and collective consciousness. In 2016, Michael Dillbeck and Kenneth Cavanaugh came to the following conclusion 'as hypothesized, there was a statistically and practically significant shift in trend in the direction of reduced rates for each of the variables beginning with the onset of the intervention period.'[1] How could we stay centered after meditation is over, and make our life a psychologically safe place for a more extended period? Where do we find those who can calm down their individually perceived world not only for a period of meditation but also to make fundamental transformations in the real world?

Meditation leads to emotional balance, and the mindfulness movement entered executive cabinets and corporate teams. Is that enough of us who could concentrate on creative pathways in the ongoing crisis? How fast could we transform, or where would we find people who could work countless

[1] Michael C. Dillbeck & Kenneth L. Cavanaugh. 'Societal Violence and Collective Consciousness' in SAGE Open, 6 (20). April 2016.

hours motivated just by the idea of making others perceive the greatness of this world? According to various data sources, there are 400–600 million entrepreneurs across the globe, which is 5–7% of the world's population. According to Global Entrepreneurship Monitor's survey, which conducted research in 50 different economies worldwide in 2021–2022, entrepreneurial activity increased during the pandemic. However, not all entrepreneurs drive a passion for enhancing the world's greatness. Some just survive, so how many of them are motivated by money? Thankfully, the answer registered less than 30%. That data confirms my first degree dissertation research results back at the conference, which I described in Chapter 2, where I learned that empaths could feel threats the same way as they could feel opportunities. The entrepreneurial mindset is more than a money-making machine, it is about the opportunity to see gaps and serve them for others. Be creative and innovative. Entrepreneurs are small, therefore fast. They are fragile, therefore keep searching for support and supporting others. They must be sensitive yet know how to transform reality around. World change needs speed, and this is the force ready for it. Imagine what we could do if this force could be emotionally empowered.

# Chapter 9

# Sensitivity

*Gift of sensitivity and what it means*

## What is it about becoming sensitive?

The most significant benefit I gained from emotional processing, besides simply feeling good more often, was that I worked out my sensitivity. It has become my source of confidence for two reasons: it has given me the ability to foresee threats and the ability to be prepared, feeling opportunities and being ready to catch them. Life always brings us challenges; some situations are hard to be in. People gain confidence by different methods and stick to a few that work best for them, usually for a whole lifetime. For example, I was told a story by a person who saved his family member just by being able to pay for his operation at the moment of need. His belief became 'money is the solution,' so he developed himself as a good businessman, making money nonstop and teaching others how to do that. Money became his source of confidence. Another person checked on others all the time, calling people she hadn't seen for ages. It happened that I asked her why she did do so. 'Imagine you are in the city and lost all your belongings; how would you help yourself if you don't know anybody around?' was her reasoning. Social connections had become her source of confidence.

These two examples of money and social connections are based on the need for security and serve as an example of external solutions for self-confidence. Sensitivity is our inner ability, and this source of confidence is based on individually curated safety; nobody can take it from us. I think external and internal solutions are both needed. Both work best together; safety and security go hand in hand. We must take care of ourselves; therefore, a reasonable level of external solutions must occur in our lives. We cannot rely on them for the long term as changes come. It must be an inner source of confidence that lets us know we can find a way through challenges. That is why sensitivity becomes an established, recognized, and empirically verified human trait. Sensitivity enables us to foresee situations on the evolutionary path, especially if it connects with a group or community and is necessary for protection. Sensitives are the best guards of protection and alarm.

Sensitivity also becomes an evolutionary response helping us to navigate the social world with a unique understanding of others through emotional empathy. Sensitives understand others' emotions, situations, life circumstances, what troubles them, and what kind of energy is around them. I think different people develop different sensory channels of sensitivity. For example, I am very sensitive to voices, which could give me much more information about the person. I also could remember a voice for a long time, although I would forget how the person looked, what their name is, and what circumstances we met in. Sensitives usually forget a lot because they process so much information, so it's impossible to remember details. To my mind, the essence of another person is their voice, so I remember that information.

Sensitives use precognition to solve societal and scientific tasks, and many feel and express the beauty of art. You may think that only certain people have that ability, but you can develop sensitivity through emotional processing. Once we process emotional layers, we become more and more sensitive. Access to sensitivity comes naturally to any of us once we pass by tidal waves of unprocessed emotional baggage. Sensitive people also always have 'a different view on things,' recognize patterns, and see invisible connections.

## As with any gift, sensitivity needs practice and curation

As with any other ability, sensitivity requires curation; this is the path I have been exploring for eight years. We need to process emotions, and then the external world will organize itself. We are still involved in situations, yet the time factor is less. Time is our most pressured resource, so why don't you try this way? Sensitivity works because high emotional states save time for unhealthy resistance and reactions yet allow adaptation following possibilities. They could bring a solution that you couldn't even think about. I'm not too fond of a routine for every day; therefore, it is a great pleasure to pick up something new that will pop up.

The process of emotional work could be organized as follows. We get the experience and feel emotions that need to be worked out. I used to do emotional work without any external experiences; releasing any emotional tensions connected to my request works the same. However, the best outcome is related to energy charge, so we must ensure we are emotionally charged or engaged during the session. Without emotional engagement, work could not be done. We sit to concentrate on bodily sensations, catch emotions, and follow through all emotional baskets witnessing and acknowledging emotions, feeling them, experiencing them, and giving them space in our hearts. It is often the case that pieces of memory come out during a work process. These are moments that are emotionally engaged with past experiences.

When direct knowing is hard to process, we visualize something through a metaphor. As I described earlier, emotions could be inherited or picked up from others. The good thing is that there is no meaning in situations, episodes, or details per se. We should concentrate on emotions and sensations. Please be aware that emotional work could be heavily charged, so starting your journey with a qualified specialist, psychologist, trauma therapist, or certified coach is strongly recommended. Once the most vulnerable layers are removed, we can do the work individually.

I experienced a great example of a Buddhist practice known as 'vipassana,' when groups or individuals sit for emotional work all together with the same intention. The approach to work is different in detail but serves as a sample where people could be involved in meditation or spiritual practices of emotional cleaning by various methods. I found my best way; your task is to find yours. With practice, you will be able to feel nuances in such a way that some techniques suit some requests best. Sometimes we want to experience something particular, just as a sensitive body would ask for a specific food, knowing what would serve it best. I remember I stayed with holotropic breathwork at the beginning of my search for about two years because this method let me experience emotional release for situations to which I have no conscious access, could not remember, or even imagine. I could shift perception without access to visuals just by senses, which works perfectly without even mind involvement.

Some emotions are hard to recognize at first, and some are very heavy to feel. For me, the pain was the longest emotion I had ever experienced. It appeared in almost all of my sessions and was hard to process. Vulnerability doesn't necessarily mean we experience much more than others; some of us could experience wounds to a higher degree than others. Therefore, sensitivity would still be perceived as a weakness. People often mix sensitivity and vulnerability. However, my task was to become sensitive without being vulnerable. Many think being sensitive is being too helpless, over-reactive, and easily overwhelmed, but it is not the case.

Sensitivity means sensing any tiny nuances of anything, especially if we pay attention to it. It also means being empathetic towards others in terms of emotional empathy, which is the ability to feel for others and not just the cognitive ability to understand what they feel. That could be applied to a sensitive person, which is very accurate. It is not a rare case for sensitive people to feel the abyss of drama, misunderstanding, loneliness, and so on.

The good news is that this could be worked out because our inner sky always has a rainbow of emotions, not only the dark side. Emotional polarities could be transformed in such a way so we would have access to the entire emotional keyboard, sensing light emotions, without drama and heaviness of trauma, in all their brightness and service to us. When we have no more emotional tensions in sessions, we upgrade our sensitivity and work out tidal waves of emotional baggage. At this moment, another level opens where we could shift attention to inward energy transmission. This is the next level of emotional work.

## What are the side benefits of being sensitive

I want to name a few side benefits of being sensitive which may inspire you in your quest for emotional mastery. It serves me best, so I would like to share my best with a deep understanding that it has transformed my life so could yours.

Not all of these I experienced; some were borrowed from friends and colleagues. People have different experiences with their sensitivity, and I trust it depends on inner intentions. I remember that from my early childhood, I asked why people behaved this or that way, especially if something hurt me. So, in my case, that question became a driver, and I can see the cause and effects of behavioral aspects. I still have that personal notepad page, which reminds me that I asked to understand cause-and-effect relations and my thunderstruck comment sometime later, 'oh my goodness, thank you, I feel it!' Practice brings more clarity and experience to polish it in time, but I am still amazed by every single session of how it works. I feel endless gratitude for that. Please, find a summary of what sensitive people say, what it is to be sensitive, and how they describe what becomes possible for them (and ready for you). Sensitive people:

1. are highly alert to external information and have a higher ability to perceive subtle changes;
2. are faster connected to nature and natural objects, recharge;
3. feel what needs for their body, health, nutrition, cure, and similar;
4. understand the hidden language of the body, so what could explain the meaning of health problems and symptoms;
5. have excellent intuition and abilities to develop it further until qualified predictions;
6. have high acceptance because they could feel all sides involved and explain their behavior;
7. find that inner peace and harmony are much easier to achieve, and time efficiency in handling reactions;
8. understand the motives and behavior of others, and scenarios others play, naturally 'reading' other people;
9. have the ability to get information much faster, and often need to check themselves for not being seen as rude because they tend to speak, interrupting others or answering the half-asked question;
10. often do something even without being asked yet, feel what is needed, and must train themselves not to be used for that;
11. find that being different could lead to disconnections and loneliness if they are still in a place of polarization/ judgment;

12. take more time making decisions, and can feel overwhelmed when asked to complete an adamant one;

13. find that their confidence grows once they start to act in accordance with their inner nature and not against it;

14. have the ability to connect with an inner understanding of anything;

15. sometimes use precognition abilities for a living, being involved in different sorts of predictions/pattern recognition, such as finance brokers;

16. significantly ease communication and prevent tensions;

17. have strong problem-solving abilities;

18. find it easy to obtain clues;

19. are very good at solving communication problems;

20. find that the more they are aligned with themselves, the easier it is to express themselves, just like art is an expression of oneself which is better once the artist is deeply connected with their core;

21. find that the more sensitive they are, the faster it is to feel opportunities of what is needed – this is not easily explained to others; if they trust themselves and stay attuned to what is their own truth, they usually get better results even without logical explanations;

22. need to train themselves to trust their inner impulses even if they can't explain them with logical reasons;

23. could experience difficulties in having their own opinion because they are natural sponges, which is very confusing, and they could see themselves 'being

jelly,' 'boneless,' or 'without a tooth' – this situation needs mastery of emotions and polarization workout;

24. have the ability to dissolve in any culture at comfort, understanding the logic and meaning of it;

25. find that patterns become the way to perceive the world, seeing hidden connections;

26. feel synchronicities, more often understanding the hidden meaning of situations and what is going on in reality, to read life 'between the lines';

27. can be stubborn, insisting that others understand them the same way or need to serve/support their vulnerability – sensitives must take complete control and responsibility for their sensitivity;

28. need to keep themselves from 'do-goodery' and let others become masters of their own; sensitivity is a huge responsibility in this regard;

29. could feel the outcome of plans and perspectives, predict things and situations, and emotional reactions of others with a high degree;

30. need to learn how to know what belongs to them and what is theirs, the same way as knowing what doesn't belong to them and needs to be given back;

31. have high adaptability, are ready faster for any change, search for a possibilities mindset in the same way as they could live in search for trauma avoidance and hiding behavior, depends on vulnerability level;

32. could embrace the unknown because it is not blind faith for them – the unknown comes steadily by resonance which sensitives could feel in advance;

33. need to take care of the information load and become masters of stimuli regulations, not to be overwhelmed easily;

34. feel the energy and ability to do any energy work, a matter of mastery;

35. could develop an ability to face difficulties searching for an inner message without confrontation or energy spent;

36. can alter the perception of self and others, pointing to what is invisible, hidden, and not evident to many;

37. usually have good oratorical skills;

38. can not only feel emotions but transmit them to others;

39. have a low resistance to the emotional pain of others;

40. have very high abilities for compassion;

41. can often develop polymath qualities, not because they are genius but based on the ability to see similar tendencies in different fields;

42. are suitable for multidisciplinary, multitasking projects based on the ability to feel the similarity in many areas;

43. switch easily between industries in their working experience, therefore having a fresh and broader perspective;

44. very often have the urge to get new information, new people, new experiences, new travels, new places, new jobs, and similar, which would create emotional engagement;

45. have strong feelings towards justice and find it easy to feel anger in situations of inequality;

46. find that cause-and-effect-relationships reading make them consider the long-term consequences of their actions;

47. have an overall understanding, acceptance, and level of love.

The list could be endless, but I hope I adequately convey the sense of what it means to be sensitive. I don't know if this is the path for everybody. Still, sensitive abilities could be developed to some extent by many, and each of us could benefit from it simply by the absence of emotional hassle and drama in which we are usually involved. I trust life has many more exciting things to be explored than just emotional peaks and reactions, although it is interesting to test. I also want to underline that it is all possible without chemicals or plant medicine. I accept and understand plant medicine, yet I believe we may achieve any state we want without it. It is an issue with the popularity of plant medicine, which used to be sacred and preserved for specially trained and prepared/leveled people. It was accessible for wise people and had a good reason for altered perception travels to be meaningful, safe, transformative, and beneficial for most.

# Chapter 10

# Vulnerability

*When I am weak, then I am strong*

## When we get emotionally unfrozen and process our emotions, we have easy access to any of them without vulnerability

The one mastering sensitivity becomes a seeker of physical tensions, which embodies emotional attachments to situations. It is so because through attachments, we have access to emotional patterns and actions we tend to implement in response to a situation. If we want these patterns to be released, we need to get access to them within our bodies. Therefore, we seek a physical sensation that holds a moment with a significant emotional charge.

A fascinating fact for me is that we don't need to return to any unpleasant details of the experience; experience doesn't matter at all. All we need for emotional processing is to experience emotions but not recall or share details of the past. Work starts only when we shift focus on emotions entirely and disconnect from any other information. Do you understand how irrelevant my concerns were regarding the inability to explain or suggest advice in the situation I described earlier with a gray cardinal character? Traditional psychology would assume sessions about experience details with detailed analysis, which could be done only by experienced professionals. However, emotional processing doesn't need a detailed conversation; it is different. My personal life experience, knowledge, or ability to give advice were irrelevant to the processing of emotions. I was laughing and embracing myself once I understood how much I tend to fear the unknown. How big were the shadows I imagined into existence through misunderstanding my sensitivity. This was the colossal lesson of my life.

Working on emotional attachments, I became concerned about how life would become after processing. I was afraid I would end up in gray, colorless flatness with no significant peaks. Thankfully, this is not so. For example, in the polarity of 'love-and-hate,' the only place that makes you feel neither love nor hate is in the middle, but this is not the way through. When we understand that real love cannot be polarized at the same frequency as hate, we get the idea that it must be dependency which we believe was 'love,' giving us so much pain. Love never gives you pain. The solution would be to leave this polarity. Love resonates much higher, and it has many more colors in it. Please never be afraid to get 'a shadow life' without lower-level polarity peaks – get rid of them freely.

When we absorb a lot of unprocessed emotions, we end up feeling the most charged of them, such as anger or pain. It is useless to work at the level of these emotions. We need to deconstruct anger or pain in such a way so we can feel all basketed emotions that lead to anger or pain. I recently read an interesting case implemented in the Netherlands. More and more Dutch people use so-called 'smash rooms' to take out their frustrations on inanimate objects. The article says, 'with anger rising for various reasons, people are increasingly visiting the locations where furniture could be broken into pieces, and glasses can be thrown against the wall.'[2] This example serves as emotional recognition and a physical way to relieve an 'extra dose.' However, being used regularly, it could create a loop where anger will require physical relief. Who knows where and under what circumstances?

The transformation of anger and the use of its energy seems to have a more ecological approach where we process other basketed emotions lying underneath the anger. Depending on the circumstances, it took time. In my case, I was working on the emotion of a broken heart, a pain, without any understanding of details causing such a high level of it, for about two years. Later I recognized grief and sorrow. It should not always be the case; average emotion processing takes about 40 minutes. Once we clean our emotional bodies, we can feel them in more nuances and access these suppressed emotions more effortlessly. Emotions that lose their arousal become much lighter and usually don't connect with physical sensations. It is a good feeling when you can say, 'I feel pain,' almost only knowing it but without a dramatic body response – a clear sign of a good job done.

Shortly after recognizing the dominating emotion, we could realize baskets of emotions and actions that we hold as bodily actions without the ability to express them.

[2] 'The Dutch Go Wild in "Smash Rooms"; Popularity Due to Energy Crisis and Housing Market,' *NL Times*, 26 November 2022. Available from: https://nltimes.nl/2022/11/26/dutch-go-wild-smash-rooms-popularity-due-energy-crisis-housing-market [accessed June 2, 2023].

## My path to emotions and a way to connect with them was meditation

I must admit here that I am writing for cases that could be considered as the medical norm only. I have no information about emotional processing by people with registered psychological disorders or any other diagnosis; doctors should have a look at such cases. I share my path to serve as an inspiration for inner work, for which you have complete responsibility. During my sessions, I checked body responses such as pain, heaviness, tears, and concentrated on emotions. Still, I also used neuroscience tools available to the public to measure my brain waves, psychological safety, or level of emotional engagement. Registered feedback information, be it in meditation or connection to particular states, is a perfect way for researching and training.

My meditations started with the sensations in the body. I tried different ways: feel what is most needed or navigate body sensations in a desired order without priority to places. Any of these methods work. Reaching actual blocks of emotions is possible by being disciplined in the way you want. The beauty of the process is that we always get a response from a body and connect with situations through emotional engagement. This engagement helps you recognize that you are at a suitable workplace. Emotions and senses of the body are crystal-clear signs you are 'all in.'

Some people ask: what if we imagine ourselves as something that has no place or relevance? Well, it could be the case, yet I consider our body a book, ready for us to read. If we have images without emotional engagement, this is a clear sign we are dreaming and not doing work. Mind visualizations are useless and empty if we have no emotional engagement and don't feel emotions. Any responses, such as senses and emotions, show it is real. Remember, what is real for our perception is enough for work.

Sometimes I felt a need for work to be done but could not become emotionally engaged or could not go through a single emotion. In this case, I set the intention for additional information needed. We can obtain information in various ways, such as by meeting new people, experiencing particular episodes, or pointing out something that will grab our attention. In this case, we can set a question, and the answer will come almost automatically. If we are ready to receive information, we will always get it; it matters to stay open.

Some say they would ask their guides for help or consult with angels, and many sensitive people live in those realms. I find it beautiful and accept whatever we perceive as real. In my case, I had no connections with any beings except humans in my life. However, I am open to any experiences. I don't see visuals like mediums and don't have manageable out-of-body experiences. Information usually comes to me via meditation or a simple internet search. However, being in a flow, I often cannot explain how I started a search about Manchester, yet arrived at Liverpool. I also could get inner knowing without anybody telling me things; individual sensitivity experiences are very different. We could use the benefits of our abilities without a detailed understanding of how it works. More important is that it helps us feel good, healthy, and happy.

When we practice our emotions, we must not polarize reality but feel the spectrum. It was very soon after the start of my emotional work that I could identify dualities or polarities following the ability to sense where contraction happens. The next level is work that can be done with the mind which is already free from emotional charge. For this reason, you may use a metaphor of a triangle with a base known as the polarity of 'thesis-and-antithesis,' which a serving solution located in the third point of 'synthesis.' However, bear in mind that synthesis is never ever being on the same frequency as polarity, if is always out of it. Once we notice polarities, we know we are about to uncover synthesis and thus sort out the situation with the tension of limiting beliefs. Thesis and antithesis both represent limiting beliefs and causing tensions. Synthesis accepts both as a relaxation point. Acceptance is the key to all.

## Mastering emotions doesn't require doing specific work – that was my choice; life supplies us with emotionally charged situations in abundance

Life supplies us with emotionally charged situations in abundance. Combining emotional practice and attention to real-life situations gives emotional liberation depth and speed. It is important not to become disconnected from real life, which is a practice in so many traditions. I know many people in unique places of power (such as ashrams) who mastered themselves for so long, but cannot, for example, use a bus without being devastated. It is an example of a false freedom state, an escape from reality. Our task is to feel good and feel the best with an opportunity to solve whatever happens. One should understand and feel all actors in a given situation. This possibility comes if we stop being polarized by false spirituality and let acceptance, understanding, and love change our essence so that we don't judge or feel negative about ourselves or others.

Emotional liberation allows us to resonate differently with the outer world, which serves as a reflection or mirror. Once we know, accept, and neutralize our emotions, miracles happen. Our limiting beliefs, motives, and undesired behaviors, such as judgment, often dissolve by themselves. There would often be no need to think in urgency, 'oh, I am in a judging position right now,' and stop yourself via control. You won't have these situations at all.

Emotional work could be done via art and processing by connection with the feelings of others, based on empathy. Such work could include the use of theater plays, cinema production, music or visual arts, literature – anything which engages our emotions. You can imagine how helpful my love for books was, through which I have learned so many characters, behaviors, and situations, feeling them being deeply sensitive. This information was beneficial to the unprepared heart.

The vital information about anything we try to achieve by control is that all that is suppressed will return with a higher degree or intensity. Thus, it is useless to use stoicism practices without being stoic by nature. We are dependent if we want something and practice rejection while still being emotionally super-attached to it. Any attachment could be stopped by willpower and control; rejection is a perfection. It could even be a great pleasure to feel your power of will and know that this is you, who decides if you want to choose something or not. But the art of non-attachment wouldn't be in rejection and control. It is the ability to dissolve a catchy desire itself, not to get protection over it or know how to handle it.

Vulnerability can be released excitingly. Resistance or walls of protection will not do it. You can remove it by dissolving the hooks of emotional attachments inside. Once you become neutral, or vacuum-like empty, any super-charged emotion goes through without staying for long. The less vulnerable you become, the faster you recover from defensive reactions. It happens by emotional processing and healing of traumas; this is the first direct effect I gained. All acceptance, polarization work, and other discoveries happened later.

The first target is to work out vulnerability so that all emotions become available to us without extremes caused by attachments. An emotional attachment causes vulnerability, yet emotional engagement is the type of connection norm. Without vulnerability, you could experience sensitivity differently. It was a huge relief even to know about that. Scientific research confirms that highly sensitive people cannot become less sensitive. However, senses cause emotions, and it is possible to manage emotions where we get sensitivity in nuances that don't bother us. All environmental stimuli without emotional polarization will become lighter. They will not emotionally abuse you anymore. One day it became like a noise that didn't influence me, simply existing around me just as trees or flowers do, to which only I decided to pay attention. A healed vulnerability has a side effect of an open intuition channel, which the one who practices sensitivity has the best access to. Intuition is the direct result of cured sensitivity.

## We behave very similarly in survival, and there are not so many scenarios

The last piece of emotional work is to find saving beliefs that limit current life; thus, all levels become accepted – emotions, body response, and mind beliefs. Once you become conscious about, understand, see, experience, and feel the scenario you have been attached to, it will disappear from your life. Beliefs must be reconstructed to be more suitable for what is ongoing now.

Two important notices. Any work should follow the exact request. I have seen many people in ongoing work without significant personal life changes. It happens because they don't serve themselves with direct intentions. People do cleaning work for families, friends, and anybody else; this sounds so important to them. Yet, we can only help others once we emotionally stabilize ourselves first. Also, working for others helps when you remember that it has a connection to your situation. For example, it could be your current situation when a client comes with the same pattern. Or it could be your past experience, which was worked out and, therefore, relevant to you. Whatever we are sorting out must be personal and about your life. Emotional work is not the work of healing others, this work is for your energy field, for your own emotional state. There are situations when we could help others, but, in this case, we only hold the space for the one doing the work.

I understand, see, feel, and 'know' the cause and effect of many relations which bring so much clarity to my life. Some situations are workable, but with some, we need to go through them. Yet, if you know this information, it is much easier to navigate. I meet people who experience and work similarly, so it seems this type of work is available for all – there is nothing unique in it. Direct intention and an open heart could do anything and everything in love. If I was able to make this happen, so could you.

# Chapter 11

# The Curation of Life

*You should never disconnect from your emotions,*
*especially making important life or business decisions*

## Manage the situation, or the situation will manage you

'Do it, stop being emotional, take back control, move, and don't get stuck' – all of these are so familiar to many of us. I was 'in control' for half of my life using the way of personal influence. It worked out until I collapsed. People try to influence real life through mental decisions and emotional disconnections. How many times I have heard about keeping a 'cool head' and could not agree more! For sure, making any decision from emotional reactions would be self-distracting. However, we usually suppress emotions to connect with a 'cool head' logic. I was even trained in that in business seminars.

It is working, yet causing burnout. Once we devalue our feelings and prioritize our own decisions, it works as an elastic band that will be pulled back at the moment of highest tension. In this case, we often face health problems because the physical level is the last point that shows that we destroy ourselves. Some of us do it steadily, and some burn fast. Have you ever heard of 'good people who leave us so fast'? People who are good to everybody around them often do it at the expense of their own self; therefore, burnout happens faster.

Emotional disconnections are helpful for a situational cold shower, and you may put them aside or align with yourself through a short meditation. It helps like a bypass; however, it doesn't save us, but gives us some extra time. Later, we will need to come back and work out what was so emotional for us. In some cases, it could be minor feelings; in other cases, it could be quite deep. However, if we escape from ourselves, we use our energy 'in advance,' borrowing it from future happy moments.

## Disconnections work at the expense of your life resources

Life is our only teacher, and no masters, gurus, or external authorities can be superior to simple, everyday, mundane life. Nothing could be more spiritual than your everyday experiences. Once we disconnect from emotions, we lose the message and our connection to life as a teacher. We start to believe we are here to make wins in experiences and learn from experiences about how to act better. However, our task is to feel good before, after, and during any experiences in life. Feeling good is the primary outcome that supports our health, level of life, and level of energy. Many of us think that a lifestyle, these little beautiful things available for us for a particular amount of money, give us long-term life satisfaction. However, many understand that the level of energy and health, quality of our connections, and opportunity for self-expression would be quite a solid alternative to any material lifestyle and do not require money at all! The truth is, we could do whatever we want, mastering emotions to feel good, whatever happens. We could feel truly good, without the necessity to lie to ourselves or others, or play in positivity, just feeling good, being in harmony within. My life changed so much once I understood this.

When you feel good about something, it is good for you, it means you are emotionally engaged. We have an internal compass that shows us what it is to feel good. Even though sometimes we feel great defeating someone unpleasant to us, we know that revenge will not bring us back to what we lost and value, what was important to us. These post-actions towards others don't change the situation and don't make us feel good even if we believe it was the right thing to do. The task is to feel good, not to feel right. We disconnect from ourselves if we do something and don't feel good about it. In my case, all life that I built on disconnections collapsed.

I found from other people that many who faced primary, extreme life situations would recall how boring, mechanical, repetitive, and lacking in positive emotions their life was just before the dramatic episode. A life flow works in such a way that we usually don't face drama without being informed about it. Some people would say, 'oh, no, life was so good, and then suddenly it happens.' Well, all situations are different. In many cases, life seemed comfortable because we closed our eyes to the reality in attachments, choosing to limit perception, favoring this blinkered way. It gives comfort and gives us stability and psychological safety, yet it could work as a comfortable swamp preventing any changes and personal development. Once we stop mastering our brilliance and stop developing ourselves, we get feedback on where to focus our attention. Even if we do not study at school, do not achieve the highest possible career post, do not have a marriage, or be famous on social networks, we still could have a happy life. However, we will learn lessons if we stop self-development and collect negative emotions. Life is a flow; if we don't move or change, we start to die.

Our job is to listen and take action accordingly; thus, we could be in line with a life flow. I call that process a curation life. It is not managing life circumstances, but curating or mastering our own life in a way so that we make sure our outer world reflect our inner beauty, which we process, clean, and take care of.

In my case, life was bright until I was driving my red sports car to a 'happy life' definition and stopped being so shortly after I achieved a desire. This happy life image was my motto, my dream, a visual in my head that I wanted with my heart. It lost its colors, and I could not understand for quite a long time what I did wrong if this was what I wanted so much. Steadily gaining understanding from my sessions, others' experiences, wisdom, and knowledge from people and books, I finally get it and will share with you a case.

## Emotional clouds

The reason connects to the moment I took that 'happy life' decision. It was precisely a moment when I felt an 'emotionally clouded heart.' I created the term 'emotionally clouded heart' because I faced many situations when I was perplexed by the outcome. I asked my heart, and I felt it was 'mine.' I connected with it, yet kept getting life's slaps. Many of them made me cautious with heart-based decisions, and I started to collect hints. My target was to gain a clear connection with myself, without doubts or results, which would be back-ordered. I wanted to understand myself and why the realization of my dreams and wishes didn't make me happy. I believed in good intentions and support of life, so deep within, I didn't question my abilities to get correct results. Yet, I had the inner feeling that I didn't understand something, could not get the message, and didn't break through.

As a result, I found that my heart was clouded by emotions and had no emotional clarity. I found myself being full of solutions I created from my life dramas. For example, we never had enough money; therefore, I built a desire to earn it and could make it quite successfully. However, the money went just as easily as it came, and this wish always needed some 'stock fillers.' These fillers were not like in a normal life flow. It was always kind of a small battle and won following the necessity for that which I desired to have back. I experienced my power to achieve the solution for my need again and again. The same story, I had no complete family; therefore, one day, I declared to myself that I would be able to build it despite anything. It was understandable and very logical, but once I achieved it, my dream life fell apart. Logic is not what drives our personal life forward. I did not feel good about people, situations, or things I invited or brought into my life.

I connected my decisions to the heart, so there was no lie to myself. This understanding gave me some relief. The only matter was that I had a broken heart. That means I decided from a position of trauma. Any of my intentions saved me and gave me the strength and faith to achieve them, being an absolute polarity towards what I had. Once I reached this second pole, the pendulum started its way back, and my dream life fell apart, showing the truth. I achieved it, yet I was not happy. It helped me to fill the gap, but solutions don't heal traumas. I learned that any trauma-based wins would be empty. I cried like a baby once I understood that, simply releasing my childish wishes and processing all hidden pain. I spent years of my life on something I was building instead of living in the joy of every day.

Therefore, I will explain to you a 'third way of synthesis.' Once we are in polarity, we don't own the game. Life happens to us despite the fact we think that we hold the solution. In polarity, we never escape from pain or achieve happiness running towards pleasure. There is no solution, no way out. If we don't step into a rabbit hole of down-spiraling emotions to sort them out, we disconnect from the self by logic to be 'in control.' However, this is not long term, even if we achieve the desired – a bitter harvest.

Therefore, we must first have an inner change in our state if we want life circumstances to follow. 'As above, so below' – I found the wisdom of life in this tiny nuance. It is evident, yet I got it only once I experienced it fully. A third way of synthesis understanding becomes a gift. When we ask, 'should I stay or should I go?' or 'should I keep a marriage or be divorced?' it shows a polarity that absorbs our attention on inner drama. This polarization, however, reveals something else important. We get involved in the theater because we don't want or have no resources to see the truth. In this case, the truth is that we need to step into self-development, because our partner is not responsible for our happiness, and the situation of being him/her with us doesn't change our inner state.

I hope my kids will be aware of that information, so they play a game with open eyes and an understanding of the rules. Indeed, they are nothing new, and when I read the teachings of sages, I feel every single word with all my skin. It is so because I lived all they explained. The only problem was that they spoke a language I could not understand. It was a metaphor that needed to become a disclosure in my life, and I am so grateful I reached the point of understanding, at least some of it.

Once understood, it saves me so much time with sessions and emotional processing. I think there is logic in the fact that some practitioners practice the same thing their whole life, because deepness brings so many nuances and is miraculously attractive. You are meant to become a master in your own life. Keep working on your energy level until the new world's excellence horizons would be open for you. I have ultimate respect for practitioners, be it attention techniques, the practice of compassion, or emotional processing. I have endless respect and gratitude because what they feel will be in the human legacy available for all of us.

Another important message is that life is always true; it is our only real buddy that will never lie. Life will always reflect our actual state and continually show us what is going on without telling us what to do next. Life never tells you what to do or which ritual to follow. Routines are essential once we get our inner sense of it through experience. This teacher helps us to have those inner experiences, be engaged, understand, and accept. Our task is to transform the state. We don't need anybody to validate our own experiences; life confirms them. We need no status, diploma, certificate, or other attributes of a knowledge ladder in this school. Wisdom is always with life. Life is our best teacher. It shows where you are quietly and innocently, with a direct message of a bold truth. All our achievements have nothing in them if our hearts are closed to love, compassion, support, and freedom. Listen to everybody, and decide for yourself. Life is only happening for you; it is yours and responds individually. Therefore, other experiences we are so greedy to obtain are irrelevant, just a clue. Keys are individual. My task is to share, and your task is to reflect.

## The curation of life

What if we could become best friends with our emotions which are the source of life energy? What if we could use this energy to foresee better opportunities? What if the world is full of potential and much better than the old-fashioned and brutal survival way of life we inherited? What if we are meant to feel, know, and understand more, transform faster, and utilize more parts of our brain? What if love, unity, acceptance, and compassion let us live life fully? Why should we suppress emotions and limit our natural states instead of giving them an entire pathway?

My initial question was how to become unstuck and move forward, as I lost my creative flow. Shortly after the book *The Artist's Way* by Julia Cameron appeared in my life, I learned the meaning of morning pages, which is nothing but a cleansing of emotions. Do you remember that I told you my way of processing is a blend of meditation and trauma therapy, but there are plenty of methods? The morning pages method lets you write down all unnecessary things you have collected inside, clean blocked channels, and get clean, creative water flow again. This exercise reveals that unspoken truth is reflected in tears and emotions. This book allows me to become an essayist and open up about another gift that covered under fears and shadows of the self.

I share this to illustrate our innate ability to become a cure. Once we connect to the self, glimpses of what is needed will always appear, and we must be ready to 'catch the tail of luck.' We need to be emotionally clean, manage attention, and concentrate on what we want, request, or wish to understand. When we focus without being clean, we get hilarious results. We can laugh at them with life together if we have enough energy. If we have not, it will be a feeling of life drama and tragedy. Feeling means the same: the situation is just the situation, and our feelings about it make it a joy or nightmare. Emotions are super essential for us. They are predispositions for the outcome.

How could we curate life so we stay on the side of life we choose? It requires moving, following the sun all the time (to use a metaphor). It requires keeping clean to allow free emotional flow. Life is the teacher which endlessly supplies moments of experiences following what we have inside; we can rely on its truth from the whole heart, and it never lies. Never disconnect, therefore, from inner listening. However, please ignore the visual actor's play in such a way, so you don't become a Muppet yourself.

Who is a curator? The curator creates, organizes, and maintains things/collections/data to support decision-making, research, and other purposes. Our role is to obtain all the information possible and be sensitive. Curators are specialists in acquiring and maintaining collections, usually in art. We curate what will precisely stay in our life. A curator is from the Latin word 'cura,' meaning 'to take care,' and they are the one who oversees. Please relentlessly watch what is in your life collection. Once it is ready, invite others to become amazed visitors to your exhibition. Don't forget to change expositions following the flow of life. The idea of 'curating experiences' turns marketers into elite gurus of our days. Why don't you just become a guru of your own life?

The curator doesn't make things happen as a manager does by planning and achieving results. They are more the one who is a 'trendsetter,' so they don't manage things. They choose what is in line with the trend and help to reveal it. A curator is the one who determines what 'mine' is and is not. They understand the current status, what to acquire, and how to develop a life. Anyone can be an artist; anyone can be a curator. A curator is a facilitator who connects people and ideas with creativity and finds a way to create a universal language between all of them. Their expertise is not about managerial know-how needed to buy and sell, to start and achieve. Curating is about having a sure way to see the information 'between the lines,' see connections between things, and understand the flow of episodes. Our role is to become a researcher, select and acquire pieces we feel good about, oversee interpretations and displays, and exhibit the magnificence of personal life collection for others.

Life will always help you understand what is yours and what is not; even if you become attached to something, it destroys what is not yours. However, nobody could take what is yours from you, for it is within you.

It is a widespread belief that we are creators of our life, and I could not agree more. However, it seems that we have many ways of how to create. Some people understand creation as an arrangement of a comfortable life with material stuff available for them or a desired social status. It is fine, but this is not a creation per se, nor a miracle we could live. Other people would think of creation as hand-made things, crafting something. The creator is not trading their lifetime in exchange for available stuff, like us. This idea has nothing to do with life creation. I believe the creator is the one who transforms time and space, seeding reality, so things materialize. They are a master of the invisible. However, I think they don't create with intentions for material things and nothing to do with the manifestation we used to know. The energy manifests in the material world; this is the rule. The creator works on energy, not forms, to witness what this energy brings back to them. What is human energy? Emotions.

The famous 2006 film *The Secret* (directed by Drew Heriot) reveals the creator's possibilities. If you watch it, you will witness a level of society and culture at the time of filming. Listening to what people want to create is very interesting. This film has many great ideas, yet based on the understanding of happy life as purely materialistic, with attributes of houses, cars, money, etc. There is nothing wrong with it once you understand how energy works. Manifestation is the application of energy – our life energy, to be precise – therefore, it will never work if energy is not enough. It is always an exchange of energy between us and the world.

Engagement is a healthy way of connecting, but an attachment is a dependency. I am not the proponent of life without material stuff; it is a harmonious part of life itself; it is life. Yet I ask you if it is possible to see the energy flow underneath any matter movements, so we understand where the flow goes and how to be in line. Abundance doesn't mean the house is full of everything, although it could be a good case. Abundance is the heart that is overflowing with the emotion of love. Mine was not; therefore, I started my search with the simple belief I would be given something as a reflection of my actual state. Do you remember saying, 'God, how greedy I am being so poor'? If we are greedy for anything, it will return as being in need. It will return if we are joyful, laugh, love, or through compassion. If we judge ourselves, it will reflect. If we feel unworthy, we will trade off our body, time, space, and skills to become worthy, which will reflect too.

However, we need faith only to keep working on our inner state with a simple understanding that the world is the energy, and so are we. I could raise my energy by borrowing it from the world (through matter), yet everything exists in balance, so I will need to give back. I could exchange as much as I wanted. Exchange is the law of life. I also could dissolve and become a flow, a path, a life, an energy which I am. I remember how I could not understand what 'I am the path' means. I was looking for a wise figure, the reason for life, meaning, or the path best fitting me. Clarity came when I felt my inner emotional world experiencing it as an energy flow. It happens by understanding how I could observe it, change it, transform it, direct it, yet how I could depend on it, be attached to it, and get vulnerable because of it with the same probability. My inner state is a predisposition to the path. The path will happen based on what we have inside. Therefore, I am the path. Life will follow your inner state without a need for manifestation. Inner emotional abundance is the true meaning of abundant life.

## Step the abundance, and abundance will step to you – become a gift, and a gift will be given

Whatever I understood would save the time of others, as had happened for me. Whatever I achieved would inspire others, as my work was inspired by a curious multitude who became embers of my enthusiasm. With deep gratitude in my heart, I want to share a few words I repeat in my meditations so you can feel me anytime. Dear reader, I hope we sit together one day to experience the power of emotions, as for sensitives, time and place don't matter.

You always have access to your energy, no matter how emotionally frozen. If you are, get unfrozen. You always feel the emotions, don't get rid of them, yet transform them to higher states. You cannot disconnect from emotions, and this is your energy source. Get engaged as much as possible. Our task is to work out vulnerability in full. Don't forget to ask in any situation, 'what for?'. What gift is in this situation, and what is waiting for disclosure? I often hide my gifts so deep within that I forget about them. Always remember it is a game of emotions, not experience outcomes. Become the observer of emotional dramas with an inner knowledge of how to release emotional baggage using the 'third position.'

Be different, uncover endlessly, as who you are is everything. At the same time, remember you are nobody, don't get attached to roles, and stay the actor. But become a brave actor, who tries different repertoire, crazy roles, heavy lines, and sparkling moments, for this is life. Fall in love with that unique ability to become whoever you want to become, yet stay centered on who you are. Would you judge your achievement knowing this personality is your creation? Don't you feel you will support it emotionally so you can move forward? Such a joy to know you could try different roles and realize endless opportunities. If you don't get stuck in circumstances with limiting beliefs, this is the maximum you can achieve. What if you stop playing the drama, simply stepping out of it with the understanding this is your personality, so you have a resource to change it?

Unplug, and let life wash away what is not yours. What if you are meant for more, much more than you could imagine? Open a wider door to life. Get wisdom from others, from life itself, and become a curator of your life collection. Take good care of what is dear to you. Think big, and master your life bravely. Don't put up blocks and barriers to love. Keep the flow of healthy curiosity, dreaming, belief rotation, faith to miracles, ability to feel and know invisible, and read between the lines. Always know life is a flow of information, situations, and data (people) where you are a tuning fork.

Please keep your flow clean, directing your perception. Any new choice liberates the past and influences the future. Let it have a spark!

Connecting to wisdom, don't throw away pearls if you don't understand them. Don't throw away anything. It is all carefully made for dear you. Please understand that other people's words are empty for you until you respond emotionally to them, so get engaged. Therefore, wisdom does not act instantly on everyone because we all have different energy levels. The proverb, 'The well-fed do not understand the hungry,' helps to understand why different levels of energy give us a different understanding of life. Therefore, the world's wisdom is useless until you reach its level.

It is a great relief to know that our emotional body has a built-in tool that helps to open a door for that level. Work step by step, with care and compassion, with the understanding that you release what is possible for your energy, with honest intention and deep knowledge that you will continue to take steps. The inner purpose is fundamental.

The world is individually perceived; some found it fantastic, yet some could barely cope. Most of us don't know that we can work out vulnerability, which should not be our partner forever. Perception is a product of your emotions. You own the power to perceive a world in clarity. This power is now due to be fully revealed in your life.

When your heart finds a way to freedom, speak it out. Sensitives come to serve the world by personal example and helping develop many. The best human potential is realized only in a community.

# About the Author

Elena is a founder, an author, a Ph.D. researcher, and a passionate advocate for human emotional potential. With over 15 years of international business and startup experience, she has led and supported multiple ventures across various industries and markets, leveraging her C-level executive background and her cross-cultural management skills. She founded Small Dots, which is developing a platform to empower people to discover and express their sensitivity, creativity, and polymathy for business, science, and art.

Elena has formal degrees in management, biology, business administration, and psychology at the Master's level and is also pursuing her Ph.D. at the University of Nicosia, Cyprus. In this work, she blends behavioral psychology and economics and applies neuroscience to study the behavioral factors that influence sustainable consumption and engagement in the Experience Economy. She is an emotional intelligence and heartfulness ambassador and a polymath who integrates Eastern and Western wisdom, business and science, and corporate and individual psychology. Amber believes that emotions are the key to both our personal and professional lives and that we have the chance to keep the beauty of life in our hands right now. Drawing on her extensive research and personal experiences, she provides a fresh perspective on what it means to be human in an age of technological acceleration, highlighting the importance of emotions.

# Index

information retrieval 31
inner guilt 126
inner resourcefulness 117
inner work 81–85, 97, 107, 110
innovation 78
innovative thinking 13
internal validation 77
introverts 14

**J**
Jonathan Livingston seagull 95–96
joy 99

**K**
Kaa the python 18
Kabbalah 58
knowledge, meaning of 116–117

**L**
law of attraction 30, 124, 126
law of flow 28–29
learning
  concept of 110
  a process of life 111
left alone 92–93, 97, 100–101
liberation 71
lies, as source of pain 10–11
life
  always true 167–168
  an everyday challenge 15–19
  understanding, and energy levels
    175
life flow 133, 163, 164, 165,
    172–173
life messages 31–33
life of dreams, becomes true
    reality 52–54
life resources, and disconnection
    162–164
limiting beliefs 60–62, 96, 97
loneliness 11, 54, 63, 80
losses, learning from 88–93

love 152
  defining 70
love-and-hate polarity 152
loving force 104

**M**
Maslow, Abraham Harold 132, 134
master, defining 130–131
mastering 110
mastery 70–71, 95, 117
  emotional 130–138
material status 8
*The Matrix* 52
meant for more, feeling of 28
  and messengers 31–33
meditation 30, 61, 69, 83, 137–
    138, 169
  and emotions, points of
    connection 154–156
  guided 73
  and the mind 156
  sensations in the body 154–156
  *see also* inner work
men, wounds of 4
mental reasoning 96
mental time travel 89–93
mental work 91
messages
  emotional response to 103–108
  hidden 112–113
messengers 31–33
metaphor 142, 156
mind, and meditation 156
mind time travel technique
    99–101
mindfulness techniques 91, 97
moment of the present 48
money, as source of confidence
    139–140
mood 126–127
morning pages method of
    processing 168–169